FREN COOKBOOK

YOUR ESSENTIAL GUIDE TO THE ART OF FRENCH HOME COOKING IN 55 TRADITIONAL RECIPES

EMMA YANG

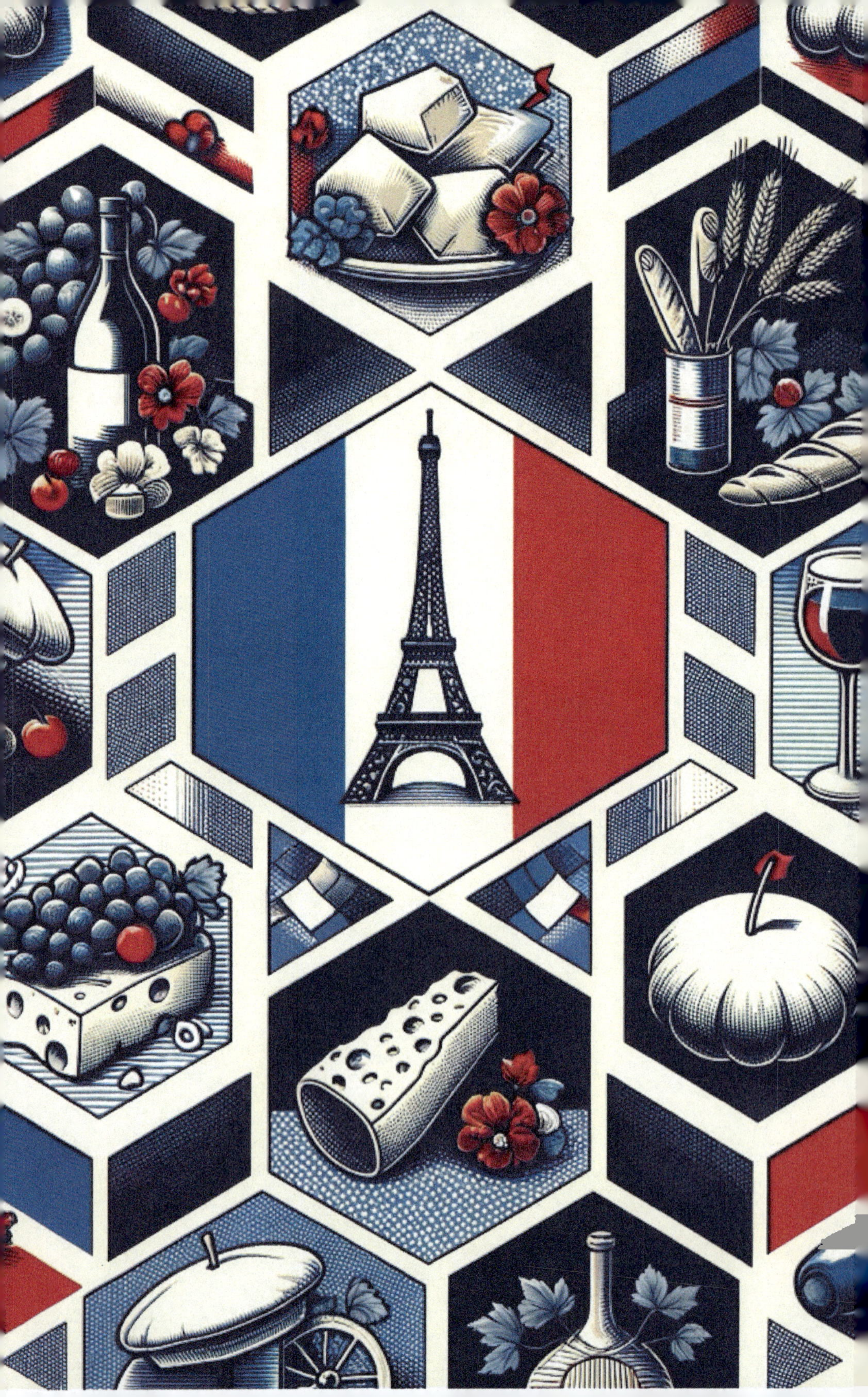

© Copyright 2024 by Emma Yang - All rights reserved.

Without the prior written permission of the Publisher, no part of this publication may be stored in a retrieval system, replicated, or transferred in any form or medium, digital, scanning, recording, printing, mechanical, or otherwise, except as permitted under 1976 United States Copyright Act, section 107 or 108. Permission concerns should be directed to the publisher's permission department.
Legal Notice

This book is copyright-protected. It is only to be used for personal purposes. Without the author's or publisher's permission, you cannot paraphrase, quote, copy, distribute, sell, or change any part of the information in this book.
Disclaimer Notice

This book is written and published independently. Please keep in mind that the material in this publication is solely for educational and entertaining purposes. All efforts have provided authentic, up-to-date, trustworthy, and comprehensive information. There are no express or implied assurances. The purpose of this book's material is to assist readers in having a better understanding of the subject matter. The activities, information, and exercises are provided solely for self-help information. This book is not intended to replace expert psychologists, legal, financial, or other guidance. If you require counseling, please get in touch with a qualified professional.

By reading this text, the reader accepts that the author will not be held liable for any damages, indirectly or directly, experienced due to the use of the information included herein, particularly, but not limited to, omissions, errors, or inaccuracies. You are accountable for your decisions, actions, and consequences as a reader.

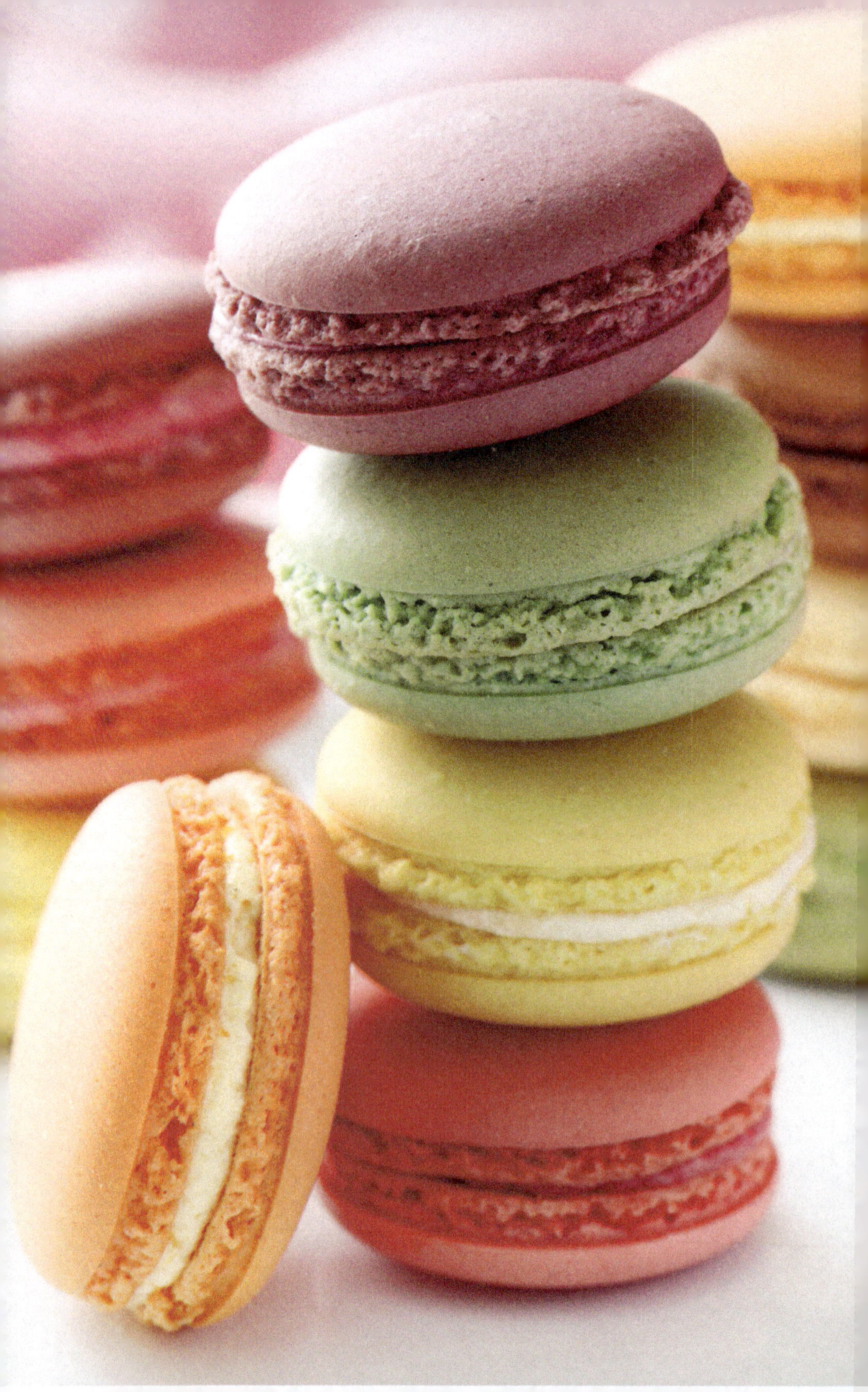

PREFACE

Bienvenue, dear reader, to an enchanting gastronomic journey that sails through the rich and sumptuous world of French cuisine. Here, within the pages of this beautifully curated cookbook, you will traverse the rolling hills of the French countryside and the bustling streets of Paris, exploring timeless classics, exploring local legends, and discovering hidden treasures—all while indulging in innovative twists that celebrate the magnificence of French culinary arts.

French fare, known lovingly as "la cuisine française," is a reverent ballet of elegance and flavor. It is here, in the delicate layers of a buttery croissant and the robust earthiness of Coq au Vin, that the essence of France is savored. Each recipe in our collection is a homage to the country's profound love affair with food, blending the meticulous techniques of chefs with the heartfelt warmth of home cooking.

Through the curated classics, like Boeuf Bourguignon and Quiche Lorraine, we whisper the secrets of time-honored traditions. Your kitchen will be filled with the heady aromas that have lingered in the bustling French markets and serene vineyards for centuries. Fresh baguettes, delicate soufflés, and sinful Crème Brûlée await to awaken your senses and transport you to a quaint bistro terrace under the shadow of the Eiffel Tower.

The 'Local Legends' and 'Hidden Treasures' seek to reveal the depth and diversity of French regional delicacies. Here, we present the comfort of Cassoulet, the soulful Bouillabaisse, the indulgence of Tartiflette, and the rustic charm of Choucroute Garnie, each dish telling the tale of the terroir from which it originates.

Our 'Innovative Twists' aims to enchant your palate and ignite creativity. The Lavender Honey Croissants and Deconstructed Beef Bourguignon are but glimpses of how classic French culinary principles can be woven into new, exciting tapestries for the modern epicurean.

This cookbook is an odyssey, mapping the intricate and delectable courses of one of the world's most revered cuisines. Beyond the harmony of flavors and impeccably tested recipes, we strive to impart the joie de vivre that is intrinsic to French dining. Our collection captures the soul of French cuisine, inviting you to revel in the beauty of creating and sharing meals that are a true feast for the senses.

Accompanying each dish, you will find narratives and insights distilled from the wisdom of French chefs and connoisseurs. We celebrate not only the sensory pleasures of each recipe but also the connections and memories forged across tables laden with love and care.

This book is not just an assembly of recipes—it is a tribute to culture, an exploration for the senses, and a paean to the art of French cooking. Whether you're an experienced gourmand or a curious newcomer to the delights of the French kitchen, this collection extends a warm bienvenue, promising a perfect marriage of time-tested authenticity and refreshing innovation.

Embark with us on this flavorful voyage, where the ancient rhythm of French cuisine meets the vibrant beat of the contemporary global kitchen, and where every bite is an intoxicating reminder of France's grand and delectable culinary landscape. Welcome, and bon appétit!

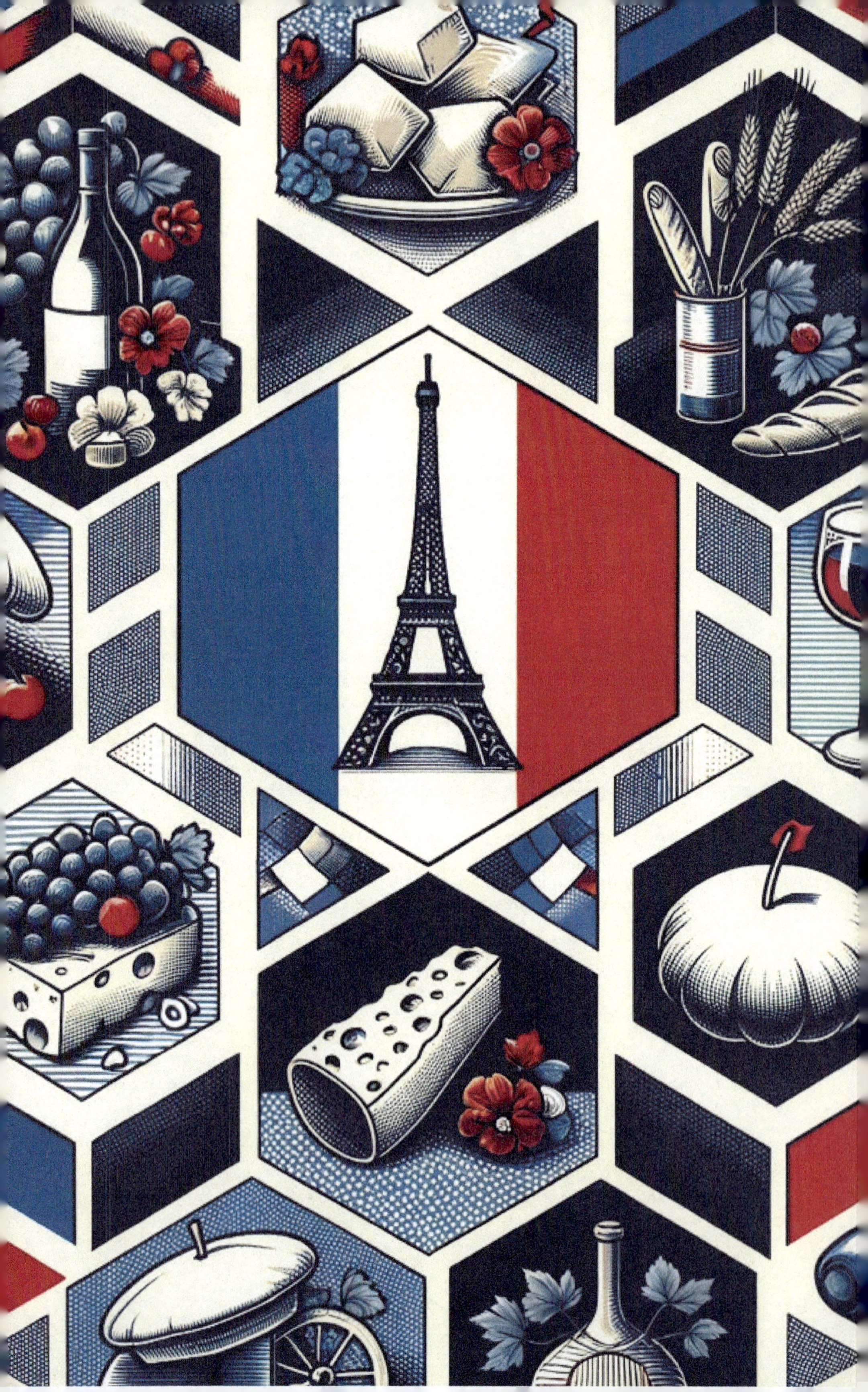

AUTHENTIC FRENCH RECIPES

CLASSIC COQ AU VIN

Coq au Vin, which translates to "rooster in wine," is a French country dish that has warmed tables with its rich flavors and succulent textures for centuries. Originally a peasant dish using an old rooster that needed slow cooking, this dish has evolved to feature chicken, braised to perfection in red wine with mushrooms, onions, and bacon. It's a culinary tapestry that combines simplicity with deep, comforting flavors.

INGREDIENTS

- 1 whole chicken (about 3-4 pounds), cut into pieces
- 1 bottle (750ml) of dry red wine (preferably Burgundy or Pinot Noir)
- 2 cups chicken stock
- 4 ounces thick-cut bacon, cut into lardons
- 10 pearl onions, peeled
- 10 cremini mushrooms, quartered
- 2 carrots, peeled and chopped
- 2 stalks of celery, chopped
- 3 cloves of garlic, minced
- 1 tablespoon tomato paste
- 2 tablespoons all-purpose flour
- 2 tablespoons olive oil
- 1 bouquet garni (thyme, parsley, and bay leaf tied together)
- Salt and freshly ground black pepper to taste
- 2 tablespoons butter (divided into two 1-tablespoon pieces)
- Fresh parsley, chopped (for garnish)

DIRECTIONS

1. Marinate the chicken pieces in the red wine for at least 4 hours or overnight in the fridge.
2. Remove the chicken from the wine, pat dry, and season with salt and pepper. Reserve the wine.
3. In a large Dutch oven or heavy-bottomed pot, heat 1 tablespoon of olive oil over medium heat. Cook the bacon until crisp, then remove and set aside.
4. In the same pot, increase heat to medium-high. Add the chicken pieces skin-side down and sear until golden brown, then flip to brown the other side. Remove and set aside.
5. Reduce heat to medium. Add pearl onions and sauté until they start to brown, then add mushrooms, and cook until softened. Remove vegetables and set aside.
6. Add the remaining olive oil and butter to the pot. Stir in the carrots, celery, and garlic. Cook for 3 minutes.
7. Sprinkle in the flour and cook, stirring, for another 2 minutes to create a roux.
8. Gradually pour in the reserved red wine, stirring constantly, then add the chicken stock. Bring to a gentle simmer.
9. Return the chicken to the pot along with the bouquet garni and tomato paste. Cover and simmer for 25 to 30 minutes, or until chicken is cooked through.
10. Return the bacon, mushrooms, and onions to the pot. Season with salt and pepper to taste, and simmer for an additional 10 minutes.
11. Remove the bouquet garni. Finish the sauce by swirling in the second tablespoon of butter to create a silky texture.
12. Serve hot, garnished with fresh parsley.

DIETARY MODIFICATIONS

Vegetarian: Replace chicken with assorted root vegetables such as turnips and parsnips, and use vegetable stock instead of chicken stock. Omit bacon or use a vegetarian bacon alternative.

Vegan: Follow the vegetarian modifications, and use vegan butter or olive oil instead of regular butter for finishing the sauce.

Gluten-Free: Substitute the all-purpose flour with a gluten-free flour blend or use cornstarch as a thickener.

INGREDIENT SPOTLIGHT: RED WINE

The spotlight ingredient for Coq au Vin is red wine. The origin of using wine in cooking dates back to the Romans, who used to cook meats in wine to preserve and enhance flavors. In Coq au Vin, the wine not only tenderizes the chicken but also imparts a distinctive, complex flavor profile that is the hallmark of this dish. The key is to use a good quality wine, as the wine heavily influences the final taste of the dish.

CHEF'S TIPS

- Marinate the chicken for as long as possible, preferably overnight, for deeper flavor infusion.
- Sear the chicken pieces in batches if necessary to avoid overcrowding, which can prevent proper browning.
- Cook the vegetables until just tender to avoid overcooking when they are added back into the dish.
- For a richer flavor, consider using homemade chicken stock and fresh herbs for the bouquet garni.
- If the sauce is too thin at the end of cooking, remove the chicken and reduce it further before swirling in the butter.

POSSIBLE VARIATIONS OF THE RECIPE

- **White Wine Coq au Vin:** Substitute red wine with white wine for a lighter version of the classic, perfect for warmer months or those who prefer a less robust sauce.
- **Coq au Vin with Pork:** Replace the chicken with pork tenderloin or shoulder for a different take on the traditional flavor palate.
- **Spicy Coq au Vin:** Add a kick by including a chopped chili pepper or a pinch of cayenne pepper when sautéing the vegetables.

HEALTH NOTE & CALORIC INFORMATION

Coq au Vin is a hearty and rich dish, packed with protein from the chicken. The bacon adds some fat, but it is moderated by the portions served. The vegetables and wine contribute antioxidants and vitamins. A serving size may have approximately 600-700 calories, with significant variation depending on the cuts of chicken used and the portion size.

CLASSIC FRENCH CROISSANT

Croissants, with their flaky, buttery layers, are synonymous with French patisserie. Their origins trace back to the Ottoman siege of Vienna, Austria, where they were first made to celebrate the defeat of the invaders, the crescent shape allegedly representing the Ottoman flag. The pastry made its way to France, where the recipe was perfected into the world-renowned treat we know today.

INGREDIENTS

- 500g all-purpose flour, plus extra for dusting
- 140ml warm water
- 140ml warm milk
- 55g sugar
- 40g soft unsalted butter
- 10g salt
- 10g instant yeast
- 250g cold unsalted butter for laminating
- 1 egg, for egg wash

DIRECTIONS

1. Combine the flour, sugar, yeast, and salt in a large mixing bowl.
2. Add the warm milk, water, and the 40g of soft butter. Mix until a dough begins to form.
3. Transfer the dough onto a floured surface and knead for 10 minutes until smooth and elastic.
4. Place the dough in a clean bowl, cover with plastic wrap, and let it rest in the fridge for at least 1 hour.
5. Meanwhile, place the 250g of cold butter between two sheets of parchment paper and pound it with a rolling pin into a square about 1cm thick.
6. Once the dough has rested, roll it out on a floured surface into a rectangle twice the size of the butter square.
7. Place the butter square on half of the dough and fold the other half over it, sealing the edges.
8. Roll the dough into a rectangle, then perform a three-fold (fold the dough into thirds). Turn 90 degrees and roll out into a rectangle again.
9. Wrap the dough in plastic wrap and chill for 20 minutes. Repeat the rolling and folding process twice more, chilling the dough for 20 minutes between each fold.
10. After the final chill, roll the dough into a long rectangle. Cut into triangles with a base around 8cm and a height of about 15cm.
11. Roll each triangle from the base to the tip to shape the croissant. Place the croissants on a baking sheet lined with parchment paper, making sure to curve them slightly into a crescent shape.
12. Cover the shaped croissants with plastic wrap and let them proof at room temperature until doubled in size, about 1-2 hours.
13. Preheat the oven to 200°C (390°F).
14. Beat the egg and brush it all over the croissants for a shiny finish.
15. Bake for 15-18 minutes until they are golden brown and puffed up.

DIETARY MODIFICATIONS

Vegetarian: This recipe is already vegetarian, no modifications needed.

Vegan: Substitute the butter with vegan block butter and use a plant-based milk like almond or soy. Replace the egg wash with a mixture of maple syrup and non-dairy milk for browning.

Lactose Intolerance: Use lactose-free butter and milk to make the croissants, and ensure the lactose-free butter is suitable for baking and laminating.

INGREDIENT SPOTLIGHT: BUTTER

Butter is crucial in creating the croissant's distinctive layers. It originated around 10,000 years ago when humans began to domesticate animals. High-quality, high-fat content butter is key as it lends flavor and creates steam during baking which separates the dough into flaky layers. The butter is equally distributed during the lamination process, which involves folding and rolling the dough several times to produce over 80 layers. This meticulous process is what gives the croissant its delicious, light, and airy texture.

CHEF'S TIPS

- Keep ingredients, especially the butter, as cold as possible to ensure the layers remain distinct.
- Do not rush the proofing stage; a slow, cool rise helps develop the flavor.
- When rolling the dough, apply even pressure and strive to maintain the rectangular shape.
- For a cleaner cut and better rise, use a sharp knife or pizza cutter when cutting the dough into triangles.
- Avoid over-egg-washing the croissants as it can prevent them from rising properly in the oven.

POSSIBLE VARIATIONS OF THE RECIPE

- **Almond Croissants:** After the first bake, cut the croissants in half and fill with almond cream, then sprinkle sliced almonds on top and bake again until the cream is set.
- **Chocolate Croissants (Pain au Chocolat):** Before rolling the triangles into the crescent shape, place a small bar of high-quality dark chocolate at the base of each triangle.
- **Savory Croissants:** Incorporate grated cheese and herbs into the dough during the folding process, and sprinkle more cheese on top before the final bake.

HEALTH NOTE & CALORIC INFORMATION

A single classic French croissant contains roughly 231 calories, with the majority coming from fats and carbohydrates. Due to its high butter content, it's rich in saturated fats. Croissants also provide a moderate amount of protein and small quantities of vitamins and minerals, particularly B vitamins from the enriched flour.

PROVENÇAL RATATOUILLE

Ratatouille is a vibrant and hearty vegetable stew that hails from Provence, a region in southeastern France known for its picturesque landscapes and rich culinary traditions. The word "ratatouille" itself comes from the Occitan language, originally "ratatolha," and has enjoyed widespread acclaim not just as a beloved regional dish but also as the star of the eponymous 2007 Pixar film. Traditionally, ratatouille is a summertime affair, prepared with fresh produce from the garden or local market. It's a celebration of simple peasant food made exceptional through the careful preparation of quality ingredients.

INGREDIENTS

- 1 medium eggplant, diced into 1-inch cubes
- 2 medium zucchinis, sliced into 1/4-inch rounds
- 2 yellow squash, sliced into 1/4-inch rounds
- 1 red bell pepper, diced
- 1 yellow bell pepper, diced
- 1 large onion, finely chopped
- 4 cloves garlic, minced
- 28 oz can of whole peeled tomatoes
- 3 tablespoons olive oil
- 1 teaspoon fresh thyme, chopped
- 1 teaspoon fresh rosemary, chopped
- 1 teaspoon fresh basil, chopped
- Salt and pepper to taste
- Fresh basil leaves, for garnish

DIRECTIONS

1. Begin by preheating your oven to 375°F (190°C).
2. Spread the eggplant cubes on a baking sheet and toss with 1 tablespoon of olive oil and a pinch of salt. Roast in the oven for 25 minutes until slightly browned and softened.
3. While the eggplant is roasting, heat 1 tablespoon of olive oil in a large pot over medium heat. Sauté the onion until translucent, about 5 minutes.
4. Add garlic to the pot and cook for another minute, until fragrant.
5. Stir in the bell peppers and cook for about 5 minutes until they begin to soften.
6. Crush the tomatoes with your hands or a fork and add them to the pot, along with their juice.
7. Add the roasted eggplant, zucchini, and yellow squash to the pot. Stir in the thyme, rosemary, and basil, and season with salt and pepper.
8. Bring the mixture to a simmer, then reduce the heat to low, cover, and let it cook for 30 minutes, stirring occasionally.
9. Uncover and cook for an additional 10 minutes to allow excess moisture to evaporate. Adjust seasoning if necessary.
10. Serve the ratatouille hot, with a sprinkling of fresh basil leaves as garnish.

DIETARY MODIFICATIONS

Vegetarian/Vegan: Ratatouille is inherently vegetarian and vegan-friendly, as it primarily consists of vegetables and herbs.

Gluten-Free: This dish is naturally gluten-free but be sure to check canned tomatoes for any additives that may contain gluten.

Low-Carb: For a low-carb version, substitute eggplant and squash with lower-carb vegetables such as mushrooms or green beans. Keep in mind, this significantly alters the classic makeup of the dish.

INGREDIENT SPOTLIGHT: EGGPLANT

Eggplant, also known as aubergine, is native to the Indian subcontinent but has settled into Provençal cuisine flawlessly. It's meaty texture and ability to absorb flavors make it a staple in ratatouille. Eggplants are rich in fiber and antioxidants. Interestingly, eggplant is a berry by botanical definition, and it was once believed to cause insanity, hence its other historic name, "mad apple." For ratatouille, eggplant lays the foundation in terms of texture and taste.

CHEF'S TIPS
- Salt the eggplant after cutting and let it sit for 30 minutes to draw out bitterness, then rinse and pat dry before roasting.
- To achieve optimal flavor, use the freshest herbs possible. Dried herbs are a viable alternative but use them in smaller quantities as they are more potent.
- Cook vegetables individually before combining them to ensure each retains its distinct texture and flavor.
- For a smokier flavor, you can grill the vegetables briefly before adding them to the stew.
- Leftovers taste even better the next day as the flavors have more time to meld together.

POSSIBLE VARIATIONS OF THE RECIPE
- **Layered Ratatouille:** Slice the vegetables thinly and layer them in a circular pattern in a baking dish on top of the simmered tomato sauce for an elegant presentation, baking until tender.
- **Ratatouille Pasta:** Toss the finished ratatouille with your favorite cooked pasta and some freshly grated Parmesan cheese for a hearty meal.
- **Spicy Ratatouille:** Add chili peppers, cayenne pepper, or red pepper flakes while cooking to introduce a warming heat to the stew.

HEALTH NOTE & CALORIC INFORMATION
A single serving of ratatouille is rich in dietary fiber, vitamins A and C, and minerals like potassium. It's low in calories with approximately 80-100 calories per cup, making it a healthy option for those looking to maintain or reduce calorie consumption. The olive oil provides healthy monounsaturated fats but should be used in moderation.

BOEUF BOURGUIGNON

Originating from the Burgundy region of France—known as Bourgogne in French—Boeuf Bourguignon is a traditional stew that embodies the rich depth of French cuisine. It celebrates a harmonious blend of beef, wine, and aromatic vegetables simmered to perfection. Allegedly favored by the duke of Burgundy, Philippe the Bold, as a symbol of the region's culinary prowess, this dish has evolved into a beloved staple in French households and a must-try for gastronomy enthusiasts around the world.

INGREDIENTS

- 2 lbs beef chuck, cut into 2-inch cubes
- 6 oz thick-cut bacon, diced
- 1 large onion, chopped
- 3 medium carrots, sliced into 1-inch pieces
- 3 cloves garlic, minced
- 3 cups full-bodied red wine, preferably Burgundy
- 2 cups beef stock
- 1 tbsp tomato paste
- 1 bay leaf
- 1 tsp dried thyme
- 1 tbsp all-purpose flour
- Salt and freshly ground black pepper, to taste
- 2 tbsp olive oil
- 1 lb fresh mushrooms, quartered
- 10 pearl onions, peeled
- Fresh parsley, chopped for garnish

DIRECTIONS

1. Begin by heating a large Dutch oven or heavy-bottomed pot over medium heat and cook the bacon until crisp. Remove bacon and set aside on a paper towel to drain, leaving the fat in the pot.
2. Pat the beef cubes dry with paper towels to ensure proper browning. Season the beef generously with salt and pepper.
3. Increase the pot heat to medium-high. In batches, sear the beef cubes on all sides until browned, about 3-4 minutes per batch. Transfer the browned beef to a plate.
4. In the same pot, reduce the heat to medium. Add the chopped onions and carrots, cooking until they begin to soften, about 5 minutes.
5. Stir in the minced garlic and tomato paste, cooking for another minute until aromatic.
6. Sprinkle the flour over the vegetables and stir until well coated, cooking for one minute to remove the raw flour taste.
7. Pour in the red wine and beef stock, scraping the bottom of the pot with a wooden spoon to release any browned bits. Bring to a simmer.
8. Return the bacon and beef into the pot. Add the bay leaf and thyme. Reduce the heat to low, cover, and let the stew simmer for 2 hours, or until the beef is tender.
9. Meanwhile, in a skillet, heat the olive oil over medium-high heat. Add the mushrooms and pearl onions, cooking until browned and caramelized, about 10 minutes.
10. Once the beef is tender, add the caramelized mushrooms and onions to the pot. Continue to simmer for another 10 minutes.
11. Adjust the seasoning with salt and pepper, and then garnish with fresh parsley.
12. Serve the Boeuf Bourguignon with crusty bread or over mashed potatoes, if desired.

DIETARY MODIFICATIONS

Vegetarian: Replace beef with a hearty vegetable like portobello mushrooms and use vegetable stock. Omit the bacon or use a vegetarian bacon substitute. The mushrooms bring a meaty texture and umami flavor that stands up well in this rich dish.

Vegan: Follow the vegetarian modifications and also look for a vegan-friendly wine. Use olive oil instead of butter for browning and skip the traditional egg yolk finish.

Lactose Intolerance: This recipe already suits those with lactose intolerance, as traditional Boeuf Bourguignon does not contain dairy. Ensure to check the bread served with the dish or use lactose-free butter for preparing mashed potatoes if used as a side.

INGREDIENT SPOTLIGHT: BURGUNDY WINE

Burgundy wine is the heart and soul of this dish. Originating in the Burgundy region —renowned for both its Pinot Noir and Chardonnay—the wine's acidity, depth, and complexity famously enhance the richness of the beef. A good Boeuf Bourguignon relies on the quality of the red wine, so choosing an authentic bottle from Burgundy can transform this dish from simple to sublime. These wines are known for their terroir, a French term that signifies how a region's climate, soil, and landscape imprint a unique quality on the wine's flavor.

CHEF'S TIPS

- Browning the beef in small batches prevents steaming and ensures a beautifully caramelized crust that will impart a rich flavor.
- Traditional Boeuf Bourguignon benefits from a long, slow cooking process to tenderize the meat and concentrate flavors.
- Use a wooden spoon to scrape up the browned bits (fond) from the bottom of the pan after deglazing, which contributes to the stew's savory depth.
- For an even more refined flavor, prepare the dish a day ahead; the flavors develop and meld better over time.
- If available, fresh pearl onions are preferred over frozen for their sweeter, more concentrated flavor.

POSSIBLE VARIATIONS OF THE RECIPE

- **Red Wine Substitute:** For a lighter version, use a dry white wine like Chardonnay. The stew will have a different, delicate flavor profile but will still be delicious.
- **Different Herbs:** Experiment with fresh herbs like rosemary or sage for a twist on the classic thyme flavor.
- **Stew Add-ins:** Consider adding potatoes or chunks of turnip to the stew for a heartier one-pot meal.

HEALTH NOTE & CALORIC INFORMATION

A traditional serving of Boeuf Bourguignon is rich in protein and iron due to the beef. However, it also tends to be high in fat, mostly from bacon and the natural content in beef. Red wine adds antioxidants but also tannins and alcohol content. One serving can roughly contain 600-800 calories, depending on the portion size and additional sides. It is advisable for those watching their intake to serve smaller portions and increase the ratio of vegetables to beef.

CLASSIC QUICHE LORRAINE

Quiche Lorraine originates from the Lorraine region of France. It is a savory, open-faced pastry crust with a filling of savory custard and pieces of bacon or lardons. The name 'quiche' is derived from the German 'kuchen' meaning cake, which reflects the blend of German and French cultures in that region. Over time, it has become a versatile dish enjoyed across the globe for breakfast, lunch, or dinner.

INGREDIENTS

- 1 9-inch pie crust (store-bought or homemade)
- 8 slices of thick-cut bacon, chopped
- 1 large onion, finely chopped
- 4 large eggs
- 1 1/4 cups heavy cream
- 1 cup grated Gruyère cheese
- 1/4 teaspoon ground nutmeg
- Salt and pepper to taste
- Butter or cooking spray to grease the pie dish

DIRECTIONS

1. Preheat the oven to 375°F (190°C). Grease a 9-inch pie dish with butter or cooking spray.
2. If using a store-bought crust, prepare the crust according to package directions. If making homemade pastry, roll out the dough on a floured surface, then place it in the pie dish. Trim the edges and use a fork to prick holes across the bottom.
3. Place the crust in the preheated oven and bake for 10 minutes to partially cook it. Remove from oven and set aside to cool slightly.
4. In a large skillet over medium heat, cook the bacon until crisp. Remove the bacon with a slotted spoon and set aside on a paper towel to drain.
5. In the remaining bacon fat, sauté the chopped onion until translucent, about 5 minutes. Remove from heat and set aside to cool.
6. In a medium bowl, whisk together eggs, heavy cream, salt, pepper, and nutmeg until well combined.
7. Sprinkle half the cooked bacon and all the sautéed onions into the bottom of the crust, then pour the egg mixture over them. Top with grated Gruyère cheese and the remaining bacon.
8. Bake the quiche in the oven for 35-40 minutes until the custard is set and the top is lightly browned.
9. Allow the quiche to cool for several minutes before slicing. Serve warm.

DIETARY MODIFICATIONS

Vegetarian: Substitute the bacon for a mixture of sautéed mushrooms and spinach. Use the same amount as you would for bacon to maintain the dish's robust flavor.

Lactose Intolerance: Use lactose-free cream and a lactose-free cheese alternative that melts well, such as a lactose-free version of Cheddar or Swiss.

Gluten-Free: Use a gluten-free pie crust as a base for the quiche, or omit the crust altogether and make a crustless quiche by greasing the pie dish well and pouring the egg mixture directly into it.

INGREDIENT SPOTLIGHT: GRUYÈRE CHEESE

Gruyère cheese is a smooth-melting Swiss cheese known for its nutty, slightly sweet taste. Aged between 6 to 10 months, Gruyère becomes more assertive and complex, which adds depth to dishes like Quiche Lorraine. This cheese's melting qualities and flavor profile make it a classic choice for not just quiche, but also fondue, French onion soup, and gratins.

CHEF'S TIPS

- Use cold butter and ice water when making homemade pastry for a flakier crust.
- Blind baking the crust prevents it from becoming soggy once the custard is added.
- Whisk the custard thoroughly to ensure a smooth and creamy texture.
- Let the cooked bacon and onions cool before adding them to the custard to prevent curdling.
- Rest the quiche before serving; it allows the custard to set properly for clean slices.

POSSIBLE VARIATIONS OF THE RECIPE

- **Spinach and Feta Quiche:** Replace bacon with chopped spinach and onions, and substitute Gruyère with feta cheese for a Greek-inspired twist.
- **Seafood Quiche:** Add cooked shrimp and crab meat instead of bacon, and sprinkle with dill for a dish that brings a taste of the sea.
- **Mushroom and Leek Quiche:** Use a mixture of sautéed mushrooms and leeks for a vegetarian option that still offers a deep, savory flavor profile.

HEALTH NOTE & CALORIC INFORMATION

A traditional slice of Quiche Lorraine provides a rich source of protein and calcium, but it is also high in calories and fat, due to the heavy cream, bacon, and cheese. A single slice typically contains around 400-600 calories, with a significant amount of saturated fat and cholesterol. Therefore, it should be enjoyed in moderation as part of a balanced diet.

FRENCH ONION SOUP

French onion soup, known as "soupe à l'oignon" in France, dates back to Roman times but became particularly popular in Paris during the 18th century. It's a simple yet hearty dish that's made its way into restaurants and homes around the world, celebrated for its rich, caramelized flavor and comforting warmth. The traditional French way involves slow-cooking onions to draw out their natural sweetness before bathing them in a wine-enhanced broth and topping with a cheesy crust of toasted baguette.

INGREDIENTS

- 6 large yellow onions, thinly sliced
- 2 cloves garlic, minced
- 4 tablespoons unsalted butter
- 2 tablespoons olive oil
- 1 teaspoon sugar
- 1 teaspoon salt
- 3 tablespoons all-purpose flour
- 6 cups beef stock
- 1/2 cup dry white wine
- 1 bay leaf
- 1/2 teaspoon dried thyme
- Freshly ground black pepper, to taste
- 1 baguette, sliced into 1/2-inch pieces
- 1 1/2 cups grated Gruyère cheese
- 1/2 cup grated Parmesan cheese

DIRECTIONS

1. In a large soup pot or Dutch oven, melt the butter with olive oil over medium heat.
2. Add the thinly sliced onions and stir until they are evenly coated with the butter mixture.
3. Sprinkle sugar and salt over the onions and cook, stirring frequently, for about 40 minutes or until the onions have caramelized to a rich brown color.
4. Add the minced garlic and cook for 1 more minute, stirring constantly.
5. Sprinkle the flour over the onions and stir until the flour is fully incorporated. Cook for another 2 minutes.
6. Slowly pour in the wine while stirring, allowing the alcohol to cook off and the flour to absorb the liquid.
7. Add the beef stock, bay leaf, thyme, and black pepper. Bring to a boil, then reduce the heat to low and simmer for about 30 minutes.
8. Preheat the oven's broiler.
9. Place the baguette slices on a baking sheet and toast under the broiler until they are crispy and golden brown, about 1-2 minutes per side. Watch closely to prevent burning.
10. Taste the soup and adjust the seasoning with more salt and pepper if needed. Remove the bay leaf.
11. Ladle the hot soup into oven-safe bowls. Place one or two toasted baguette slices on top of each bowl of soup.
12. Mix the grated Gruyère and Parmesan cheeses together and generously sprinkle over the toasted bread slices.
13. Place the soup bowls under the broiler and broil until the cheese is bubbly and begins to brown, about 3-4 minutes.
14. Serve hot, being careful as the bowls will be very hot.

DIETARY MODIFICATIONS

Vegetarian: Replace the beef stock with a robust vegetable stock. Be sure to use a stock that's rich and flavorful to mimic the depth that beef stock provides.

Vegan: Follow the vegetarian modifications and substitute the butter with vegan margarine and the cheese with a melty vegan cheese alternative that browns well under the broiler.

Gluten-Free: Omit the all-purpose flour and thicken the soup with a gluten-free flour blend or cornstarch slurry. Use gluten-free baguette or bread for the topping.

INGREDIENT SPOTLIGHT: YELLOW ONIONS

Yellow onions are the star of French onion soup. With their robust, astringent flavor that transforms into a sweet caramel delight when expertly cooked down, they make the foundation of this classic dish. Yellow onions have been a kitchen staple for ages, as they store well and are versatile in cooking. Their high sugar content relative to white or red onions renders them perfect for achieving the deep, rich caramelization essential for the traditional flavor profile we expect in a French onion soup.

CHEF'S TIPS
- Take your time caramelizing the onions; patience pays off here with depth of flavor. Avoid burning by stirring often and maintaining a steady heat.
- Use a mandoline slicer for evenly thin onion slices, which will caramelize at the same rate.
- A splash of brandy or sherry can be added to the wine for an extra layer of complexity.
- For a truly golden and crisp cheese topping, grate your own cheese rather than using pre-shredded cheese which often contains anti-caking agents.
- Toasting the bread before placing it on the soup helps it maintain some texture rather than becoming too soggy.

POSSIBLE VARIATIONS OF THE RECIPE
- **Herbal Twist:** Add a touch of freshness by including a sprig of fresh rosemary or sage during the simmering process, removing it before serving.
- **Mushroom Onion Soup:** For an earthy flavor, add sliced cremini or porcini mushrooms to the onions during the caramelization process.
- **Ale Onion Soup:** Substitute the white wine with a dark ale or stout for a richer, deeper taste that complements the sweetness of the onions.

HEALTH NOTE & CALORIC INFORMATION
A single serving of this French onion soup (excluding modifications) is rich in flavor and relatively high in sodium due to the stock and cheese. It contains approximately 300-400 calories, with moderate amounts of carbohydrates from the onions and baguette, and a good proportion of protein from the cheese. The soup also provides vitamins and minerals from the onions, especially vitamin C and B-vitamins. The cheese adds calcium, but also increases the fat content, particularly saturated fat. To reduce calorie and fat content, you could use less cheese or opt for lower-fat cheese varieties.

FRENCH CRÈME BRÛLÉE

Crème Brûlée, which translates to "burnt cream," is a dish as elegant as its homeland, France. With historical debates about its origins, some claiming it dates back to the 17th century, it has become a staple in fine dining and a beloved dessert worldwide. Renowned for the contrast of its rich custard base and hard caramelized top, this dessert became particularly popular in the 1980s, symbolizing sophistication at dinner parties and high-end restaurants.

INGREDIENTS

- 2 cups heavy cream
- 1 vanilla bean (or 1 teaspoon vanilla extract)
- 5 large egg yolks
- 1/2 cup granulated sugar (plus extra for the topping)
- Hot water (for the baking dish)

DIRECTIONS

1. Preheat your oven to 325°F (160°C). Arrange four to six ramekins in a large baking dish, depending on their size.
2. In a medium saucepan, heat the heavy cream and the vanilla bean (split and seeds scraped) over medium-low heat until hot but not boiling. If using vanilla extract, you will add it later.
3. In a mixing bowl, whisk together egg yolks and sugar until the mixture becomes pale and slightly thickened.
4. If you used a vanilla bean, remove it from the cream. If using vanilla extract, add it to the cream now.
5. Gradually add the hot cream to the yolk mixture, whisking continuously to temper the eggs.
6. Strain the mixture through a fine-mesh sieve into a bowl to ensure a smooth custard.
7. Ladle the custard into the ramekins, filling them almost to the top.
8. Pour hot water into the baking dish until it comes halfway up the sides of the ramekins.
9. Carefully transfer the baking dish to the oven and bake for 40 to 45 minutes, or until the custards are set but still slightly wobbly in the center.
10. Remove the ramekins from the water bath and let them cool to room temperature, then refrigerate for at least 2 hours or up to 3 days.
11. Just before serving, sprinkle a thin layer of granulated sugar over each custard. Use a kitchen torch to caramelize the sugar until it's a deep amber color. Serve immediately.

DIETARY MODIFICATIONS

Lactose Intolerance: Substitute the heavy cream with lactose-free heavy cream or full-fat coconut milk for a dairy-free alternative. Both options provide a similarly rich texture to the custard.

Vegetarian: The classic recipe is already vegetarian-friendly. Make sure to use vegetarian-friendly sugar that hasn't been processed with bone char.

Vegan: Replace the heavy cream with a blend of coconut cream and soy milk to mimic the richness of the custard. Use a mix of cornstarch and plant-based milk as a binder instead of egg yolks, and replace the granulated sugar topping with a vegan alternative.

INGREDIENT SPOTLIGHT: VANILLA BEAN

The vanilla bean is the star of the classic Crème Brûlée. Originating from Mexico, the Totonac people were the first to cultivate it. Now grown primarily in Madagascar, Indonesia, and Tahiti, vanilla beans are the second most expensive spice after saffron due to labor-intensive cultivation. The complex flavor comes from the pod's numerous tiny seeds. In Crème Brûlée, the vanilla enhances the creaminess with its delicate floral and sweet notes, providing a perfect balance to the caramelized sugar topping.

CHEF'S TIPS
- When scraping the vanilla bean, use the back of your knife to ensure you get every last seed.
- Be careful not to let the cream boil; scalding it can cause the eggs in your mixture to curdle.
- Always strain your custard to remove any egg chunks and ensure a silk-smooth texture.
- For the water bath, use boiling water to ensure even and gentle cooking of the custard.
- Allow the torched sugar topping to cool for a few seconds after caramelizing before serving to achieve the satisfying crack when tapped with a spoon.

POSSIBLE VARIATIONS OF THE RECIPE
- Chocolate Crème Brûlée: Add 2 ounces of finely chopped semisweet chocolate to the heated cream and stir until melted for a decadent twist.
- Espresso Crème Brûlée: Dissolve 1 tablespoon of espresso powder into the hot cream for a caffeine-infused version.
- Orange Crème Brûlée: Infuse the cream with the zest of one orange and replace the sugar with honey for a citrusy, floral flavor profile.

HEALTH NOTE & CALORIC INFORMATION
A typical serving of Crème Brûlée contains approximately 300-400 calories. It is a rich source of calcium and contains significant amounts of fat and cholesterol due to the cream and yolks. It should be consumed in moderation as a treat within a balanced diet.

PARISIAN BAGUETTE

The baguette, with its golden crust and soft, airy interior, is a symbol of French culture. Originated in the early 20th century, this elegant loaf has become synonymous with French gastronomy and simplicity. Baking a baguette at home brings a piece of Parisian charm into your kitchen and offers a delightful experience with a delicious outcome.

INGREDIENTS

- 4 cups of bread flour
- 1½ teaspoons of salt
- 1 teaspoon of sugar
- 1¼ teaspoons of instant yeast
- 1½ cups of warm water (around 110°F/45°C)
- Cornmeal for dusting
- Extra flour for dusting

DIRECTIONS

Prepare the Dough:
1. In a large mixing bowl, whisk together flour, salt, sugar, and instant yeast.
2. Gradually add warm water to the dry ingredients, stirring with a wooden spoon until a shaggy dough forms.

Kneading:
1. Transfer the dough to a lightly floured surface and knead for about 10 minutes until smooth and elastic.

First Rise:
1. Place the dough in a lightly oiled bowl, cover with a damp cloth, and let it rise at room temperature until it has doubled in size, about 1 - 1½ hours.
2. Shaping the Baguette:
3. Gently deflate the dough on a lightly floured surface.
4. Divide into two equal pieces for standard-sized baguettes or leave whole for one long baguette.
5. Roll each piece into a rectangle, then fold it into thirds. Finally, roll the dough into a long, thin loaf with tapered ends.

Second Rise:
1. Place the loaves on a baking tray sprinkled with cornmeal.
2. Cover with a damp cloth and let them rise for about 45 minutes, until puffy but not quite doubled in size.

Scoring and Baking:
1. Preheat the oven to 475°F (245°C). Place a shallow baking pan on the lowest rack.
2. Right before baking, use a sharp knife to make several diagonal slashes across the top of each baguette.
3. Just before placing the baguettes in the oven, pour a cup of hot water into the shallow pan to create steam.
4. Bake the baguettes in the center of the oven for 20 to 25 minutes, until they are golden brown and sound hollow when tapped on the bottom.
5. Cool on a wire rack before slicing.

DIETARY MODIFICATIONS

Gluten-Free: Use a high-quality gluten-free bread flour blend and add 1 teaspoon of xanthan gum if it is not included in the mix. The texture will differ, but a crispy crust and chewy interior can still be achieved.

Lower-Sodium: Reduce the salt in the recipe by half for a lower-sodium version. This will slightly affect the flavor and browning of the crust but can help accommodate dietary restrictions.

Whole Wheat: Make a whole wheat baguette by substituting half of the bread flour with whole wheat flour. This will result in a denser, heartier loaf with the benefits of whole grains.

INGREDIENT SPOTLIGHT: BREAD FLOUR

Bread Flour is key in making a traditional baguette. With a higher protein content than all-purpose flour, usually around 12-14%, it provides enough gluten to give the bread the right structure and chewiness. Gluten, the protein network that forms when flour and water are mixed, is crucial for the iconic airy interior and crispy crust of a baguette.

CHEF'S TIPS

- Water Temperature: Ensure the water is around 110°F to properly activate the yeast without killing it.
- Kneading: Knead until the dough is smooth and passes the "windowpane test," stretching a small piece until it's thin enough to see light through without tearing.
- Steam: Steam in the oven is crucial for a crispy crust. Keep the door closed to trap steam during the initial baking time.
- Scoring: Use a lame or very sharp knife to slash the dough. The proper depth and angle of scoring help the baguette expand evenly while baking.
- Cooling: Allow the baguette to cool completely before slicing to finish the cooking process and develop the texture.

POSSIBLE VARIATIONS OF THE RECIPE

- **Seeded Baguette:** Add a variety of seeds such as sesame, poppy, or sunflower seeds to the top of the loaves before the second rise for an added texture and flavor.
- **Herb Baguette:** Fold in a mixture of dried herbs like rosemary, thyme, and oregano into the dough after the first rise for an aromatic twist.
- **Cheese Baguette:** Incorporate shredded Gruyere or Parmesan cheese into the dough for a delicious cheesy spin on the traditional baguette.

HEALTH NOTE & CALORIC INFORMATION

A typical baguette slice (approximately 1/24th of a loaf) contains around 100 calories, with 1 gram of fat, 20 grams of carbohydrates, and 4 grams of protein. The crust's golden color and the crumb's light texture are a testament to its simple, yet refined composition: flour, water, yeast, and salt.

ESCARGOTS À LA BOURGUIGNONNE
(BURGUNDY SNAILS WITH GARLIC-HERB BUTTER)

Escargots à la Bourguignonne is a classic French dish hailing from the Burgundy region known for its rich culinary traditions. This appetizer has graced tables since the days of Ancient Rome, but it was the French who perfected the practice of preparing snails with garlic, butter, and herbs. Often reserved for special occasions due to its elegance and depth of flavor, this beloved dish embodies the essence of French gastronomy.

INGREDIENTS

- 24 canned snails
- 24 snail shells (optional, for presentation)
- 100g unsalted butter, at room temperature
- 4 garlic cloves, finely minced
- 2 shallots, finely minced
- 1/4 cup fresh parsley, chopped
- 1 teaspoon salt
- 1/4 teaspoon black pepper
- 1/2 teaspoon ground nutmeg
- 2 tablespoons brandy or white wine
- 1 teaspoon fresh thyme leaves
- 1 tablespoon lemon juice
- Baguette slices, for serving

DIRECTIONS

1. Begin by thoroughly rinsing the canned snails in cold water to remove any brine or preservative. Pat them dry with paper towels and set aside.
2. If you are using snail shells, boil them in water for 3-5 minutes to sterilize, then drain and allow them to cool.
3. In a mixing bowl, combine the softened butter with minced garlic, shallots, chopped parsley, salt, pepper, ground nutmeg, brandy or white wine, thyme leaves, and lemon juice. Mix until all ingredients are well incorporated.
4. Preheat your oven to 200°C (400°F).
5. Stuff a small amount of the prepared garlic-herb butter into each snail shell or into the compartments of a snail dish.
6. Insert one snail into each shell or compartment and top with enough butter to fill the shell.
7. Place the filled shells or dish onto a baking sheet or ovenproof dish.
8. Bake in the oven for about 10-12 minutes, until the butter is bubbling and slightly browned.
9. Serve immediately with crisp baguette slices on the side for dipping into the flavorful butter.

DIETARY MODIFICATIONS

Vegetarian: Substitute snails for mushroom caps for a similar texture. Stuff the mushroom caps with the garlic-herb butter mixture and bake as directed.

Low-Lactose: Use lactose-free butter or a high-quality lactose-free margarine in place of regular butter. This will maintain the creamy texture without the lactose.

Gluten-Free: Ensure that the brandy or wine used is gluten-free and serve with gluten-free bread instead of a traditional baguette.

INGREDIENT SPOTLIGHT: GARLIC

Garlic is the spotlight ingredient of Escargots à la Bourguignonne. Cultivated for over 5,000 years, garlic is not only valued for its distinctive pungency and flavor but also for its health benefits, including antimicrobial properties. In this recipe, garlic is a fundamental component that imparts a rich, robust essence which is mellowed and complemented by the butter and herbs.

CHEF'S TIPS

- Ensure your butter is at room temperature before mixing to achieve a smooth, easily spreadable consistency.
- The quality of garlic can make or break this dish. Use fresh, firm bulbs with pungent aroma.
- Be generous with the herbs, as they provide freshness and balance out the richness of the butter.
- If you do not have snail dishes or shells, use a mini muffin pan as a substitute to hold the snails and butter.
- Lemon juice adds brightness to the dish. Adjust to taste, but don't omit entirely.

POSSIBLE VARIATIONS OF THE RECIPE

- **Spicy:** Include a pinch of cayenne pepper or finely diced chili in the garlic-herb butter for a spicy kick.
- **Cheese Lovers:** Sprinkle a bit of grated Gruyère or Parmesan cheese on top before baking for a crispy, golden crust.
- **Herb Twist:** Experiment with other herbs such as tarragon, chervil, or oregano for a different herbaceous note.

HEALTH NOTE & CALORIC INFORMATION

Escargots à la Bourguignonne, with its generous amounts of butter, can be indulgent. Each serving typically contains a substantial amount of saturated fats due to the butter. However, snails are a good source of protein and are low in calories. A serving (6 snails) may have roughly 150-200 calories, depending on the amount of butter used.

CLASSIC FRENCH CHEESE SOUFFLÉ

Originating from early 18th-century France, the Soufflé has long been a symbol of sophisticated French cuisine. The word "soufflé" itself comes from the French verb 'souffler', meaning "to blow" or "puff up"—an apt description of the airy transformation this dish undergoes in the oven. Typically made with a base of egg yolks and beaten egg whites combined with various other ingredients, these individual servings are a culinary balancing act, delighting diners with their light texture and rich flavor.

INGREDIENTS

- 4 large eggs, separated
- 1 cup whole milk
- 3 tablespoons unsalted butter, plus extra for greasing
- 3 tablespoons all-purpose flour
- 1 cup grated Gruyère cheese
- 1/4 cup grated Parmesan cheese
- Pinch of nutmeg
- Salt to taste
- 1/4 teaspoon cream of tartar
- Freshly ground black pepper to taste

DIRECTIONS

1. Preheat your oven to 375°F (190°C). Generously butter the insides of four 6-ounce ramekins or a single large soufflé dish and coat with grated Parmesan cheese to prevent sticking.
2. In a medium saucepan, melt 3 tablespoons of butter over medium heat. Add the flour and stir continuously to make a roux, cooking for about 2 minutes until the mixture is golden and bubbling.
3. Gradually whisk in the milk, ensuring no lumps form. Cook for another 5 minutes until thick and smooth. Season with salt, black pepper, and a pinch of nutmeg.
4. Remove from heat, and while the mixture is still warm, stir in the egg yolks, one at a time, and mix in the Gruyère cheese until melted and well-combined.
5. In a clean, dry bowl, beat the egg whites with cream of tartar using an electric mixer until stiff peaks form.
6. Gently fold one-third of the beaten egg whites into the cheese mixture to lighten it. Then, carefully fold in the remaining egg whites, being cautious not to deflate them.
7. Pour the mixture into the prepared ramekins or soufflé dish, filling up to three-quarters full.
8. Bake for 25 to 30 minutes for individual soufflés (or 35 to 40 minutes for a large soufflé) until risen, with a golden crust on top. Avoid opening the oven door during baking, as drafts can cause the soufflé to fall.
9. Serve immediately, as soufflés are best enjoyed when they are airy and puffed.

DIETARY MODIFICATIONS

Gluten-Free: Substitute the all-purpose flour with a gluten-free flour blend to cater to those with gluten sensitivities. Do note the texture may vary slightly due to the difference in flours.

Lactose Intolerance: Use lactose-free milk and lactose-free cheeses that can melt well, like aged cheeses that typically contain less lactose. They can be a suitable replacement while maintaining the creamy texture.

Vegetarian: The recipe is naturally vegetarian-friendly. However, for those avoiding rennet, ensure that the Gruyère and Parmesan cheeses used are rennet-free or use plant-based cheese substitutes.

INGREDIENT SPOTLIGHT: GRUYÈRE CHEESE

Gruyère cheese is the heart of many classic French dishes including fondue, quiche, and croque monsieur. This cheese originates from the medieval town of Gruyères in Switzerland and has been produced since 1115. Made from cow's milk, it is sweet but slightly salty, with flavor that varies with age. The cheese is generally cured for 6-9 months and its creamy, nutty taste makes it an ideal candidate for a soufflé, melting effortlessly into the base and contributing to the dish's signature richness.

CHEF'S TIPS

- Ensure all utensils are completely grease-free when beating egg whites to get the perfect rise in your soufflé.
- To check if your egg whites have reached stiff peaks, turn the whisk upside down; the peaks should hold their shape without collapsing.
- Cut a collar from parchment paper to extend above the rim of your dish if you want an extra lift and a dramatic presentation.
- Do not rush the folding process; use a spatula and gentle movements to incorporate the egg whites without losing air.
- Serve the soufflé straight from the oven to impress with its height. Delay will cause it to deflate—so timing is everything.

POSSIBLE VARIATIONS OF THE RECIPE

- **Chocolate Soufflé:** Swap the cheese for 3 ounces of finely chopped bittersweet chocolate and 2 tablespoons of sugar. This dessert version will satisfy any sweet tooth.
- **Spinach and Goat Cheese Soufflé:** Add 1/2 cup of puréed cooked spinach and substitute Gruyère with soft goat cheese for an earthy, tangy alternative.
- **Seafood Soufflé:** Incorporate 1/2 cup of cooked, chopped seafood (lobster, crab, or shrimp) and a dash of cayenne pepper for a luxurious twist.

HEALTH NOTE & CALORIC INFORMATION

A cheese soufflé is rich in protein but can also be high in fat and calories, depending on the cheese and dairy products used. Typically, one serving contains approximately 300-400 calories. It's a source of calcium from the cheese and other vitamins, such as vitamin A from the eggs. However, it should be enjoyed in moderation owing to its saturated fat content.

DUCK À L'ORANGE

Duck à l'Orange is a classic French dish, known for its rich and elegant flavors. It's believed to have originated during the Renaissance period, where the sweet and sour combination was a culinary trend among the European nobility. The dish's popularity soared in the 1960s when French cuisine became a symbol of fine dining around the world. Duck à l'Orange combines the succulent richness of duck with a citrusy, sweet and tangy orange sauce that cuts through the fat, creating a harmony of flavors.

INGREDIENTS

- 1 whole duck (about 5 to 6 pounds)
- Salt and freshly ground black pepper, to taste
- 1 orange, for zest
- 2 cups chicken stock
- 1/2 cup sugar
- 1/2 cup white wine vinegar
- 2 oranges, juiced (about 1 cup of juice)
- 2 tablespoons Grand Marnier or other orange liqueur (optional)
- 2 tablespoons unsalted butter
- Fresh orange slices for garnish

DIRECTIONS

1. Preheat the oven to 350°F (175°C).
2. Season the duck inside and out with salt and pepper. Place it breast side up on a rack in a roasting pan.
3. Zest one orange and set the zest aside. Squeeze the juice and mix it with the chicken stock. Pour this mixture into the bottom of the roasting pan.
4. Put the duck in the preheated oven and roast for about 2 hours, or until the internal temperature reaches 165°F (74°C), basting occasionally with the pan juices.
5. While the duck is roasting, make the orange sauce. In a saucepan, combine sugar and white wine vinegar over medium heat. Cook without stirring until it turns a golden amber color.
6. Carefully add the orange juice to the caramel—it will bubble vigorously. Stir in the orange zest and reduce the heat, simmering the sauce until it thickens slightly, about 10 minutes.
7. Once reduced, if desired, stir in the Grand Marnier and simmer for an additional minute. Remove from heat and whisk in the butter until the sauce is smooth. Set aside and keep warm.
8. When the duck is fully cooked, remove it from the oven and let it rest for 10 minutes.
9. Carve the duck, arrange the slices on a warm platter, and drizzle with the orange sauce.
10. Garnish with fresh orange slices and serve immediately.

DIETARY MODIFICATIONS

Vegetarian: Substitute the duck for large Portobello mushrooms. Brush with olive oil, season, and roast until tender. Make the orange sauce as instructed using vegetable stock instead of chicken stock.

Vegan: Follow the vegetarian modifications but substitute the butter in the sauce with a vegan butter alternative or a few tablespoons of olive oil to achieve a glossy texture.

Lactose Intolerance: Simply use lactose-free butter or a dairy-free butter alternative for the sauce to keep the richness without lactose.

INGREDIENT SPOTLIGHT: ORANGE

The spotlight ingredient for Duck à l'Orange is, undoubtedly, the orange. Not just any orange—it's best to use navel oranges, which are known for their sweetness and abundant juice content. Originating in Southeast Asia, the orange was introduced to the Mediterranean via trade routes. It's the balance of sweet and tart in oranges that makes them perfect for sauces and garnishes in savory dishes such as Duck à l'Orange. In this recipe, orange serves a crucial dual purpose: the juice deglazes the pan and becomes the base for the sauce, while the zest adds a fragrant aroma and bright flavor.

CHEF'S TIPS

- To ensure the duck has a crispy skin, pat it dry thoroughly before seasoning and roasting.
- Score the duck skin lightly in a criss-cross pattern; this helps render out the fat and crisps up the skin.
- Always make the caramel for the sauce with constant vigilance, as sugar can burn quickly and turn bitter.
- For an intensely flavored sauce, consider using a reduction of freshly squeezed orange juice until it is syrupy in consistency before adding it to the caramel.
- Allow the carved duck to rest before serving to ensure the juices redistribute for the most tender and moist meat.

POSSIBLE VARIATIONS OF THE RECIPE

- **Spiced Orange:** Add a cinnamon stick and a star anise to the sauce while simmering, and then remove before serving for a warm, spiced note.
- **Honey Orange Glaze:** Replace sugar with honey in the sauce for a more robust and earthy sweetness that pairs excellently with duck.
- **Citrus Medley:** Incorporate a splash of lemon and lime juice with the orange juice for a more complex and multi-dimensional citrus flavor.

HEALTH NOTE & CALORIC INFORMATION

Duck à l'Orange is rich in protein and offers a range of B-vitamins. However, it is also high in fat, particularly saturated fat. Portion control is advisable for those monitoring fat intake. Additionally, the dish contains sugar, so it should be consumed in moderation by those watching their sugar consumption. An average serving without additional sides typically contains around 600 to 800 calories, but this can vary significantly based on the portion size and specific ingredients used.

CLASSIC STEAK FRITES WITH GARLIC-HERB BUTTER

Steak frites is a beloved bistro classic that's simple yet indulgent, born in the brasseries of France. It captures the essence of French cuisine—unpretentious yet sophisticated, with a focus on high-quality ingredients cooked to perfection. Our version features a succulent steak topped with a rich garlic-herb butter, served alongside crispy golden frites.

INGREDIENTS

- 2 ribeye steaks (1-inch thick)
- 2 large russet potatoes
- 4 tablespoons olive oil, divided
- 4 tablespoons unsalted butter, softened
- 2 garlic cloves, minced
- 2 tablespoons fresh parsley, finely chopped
- 1 tablespoon fresh thyme leaves
- 1 tablespoon fresh rosemary, minced
- Sea salt and freshly ground pepper, to taste
- Vegetable oil (for frying potatoes)

DIRECTIONS

1. Start by taking the steaks out of the refrigerator to allow them to come to room temperature for about 30 minutes.
2. While the steaks warm up, wash and peel the russet potatoes. Cut them into strips about 1/4 inch thick and 3 inches long. Place the strips in a bowl of cold water to remove excess starch and prevent browning.
3. Preheat your oven to 200°F (95°C) for keeping the fries warm later on.
4. In a small bowl, mix together the softened butter, minced garlic, parsley, thyme, rosemary, and a pinch of salt. Combine until well blended, then set your garlic-herb butter aside.
5. Pat the potato strips dry with paper towels, ensuring that they are as dry as possible to avoid oil splatter during frying.
6. In a large heavy pot or deep fryer, heat vegetable oil to 325°F (165°C). Fry potatoes in batches, without overcrowding, until they are soft and pale golden, about 5 to 7 minutes. Use a slotted spoon to remove the fries to a plate lined with paper towels.
7. Increase the oil temperature to 375°F (190°C). Refry the potatoes in batches until they are crisp and golden brown, approximately 3 minutes. Transfer them to a baking sheet lined with fresh paper towels, sprinkle with sea salt, and then keep them warm in the oven.
8. Season the steaks generously on both sides with sea salt and black pepper.
9. Heat 2 tablespoons of olive oil in a large skillet over medium-high heat. When the oil is shimmering, add the steaks to the pan. Cook for 4-5 minutes on one side until a brown crust has formed, then flip and cook for another 3-4 minutes for medium-rare, or longer to your preferred doneness.
10. Remove the steaks from the skillet and let them rest on a cutting board for 5 minutes to allow the juices to redistribute.
11. Top each steak with a generous dollop of the prepared garlic-herb butter right before serving.
12. Serve the steak with a portion of the warm frites on the side, and enjoy immediately.

DIETARY MODIFICATIONS

Vegetarian: Substitute steaks with portobello mushrooms brushed with balsamic glaze and grilled until tender. They provide a meaty texture that pairs well with the garlic-herb butter.

Vegan: Use portobello mushrooms as suggested above, and make a vegan garlic-herb butter by blending together plant-based butter, minced garlic, parsley, thyme, rosemary, and a pinch of sea salt.

Lactose Intolerance: Create lactose-free garlic-herb butter using lactose-free butter or ghee, which is clarified butter with the milk solids removed.

INGREDIENT SPOTLIGHT: FRESH THYME

Fresh thyme is the spotlight ingredient. A staple in French cuisine, thyme's history is steeped in both culinary and medicinal uses, dating back to the ancient Egyptians and Romans. It's an aromatic herb with a savory, earthy flavor that complements many dishes, especially meats. Thyme is key to this recipe as it imparts a subtle depth to the garlic-herb butter, marrying the flavors and elevating the steak without overpowering it.

CHEF'S TIPS

- Allow your steak to rest after cooking to prevent the juices from running out when you cut into it.
- Double-frying the frites is crucial for achieving a soft interior and crispy exterior.
- Use a thermometer for the oil to ensure the correct frying temperatures.
- Dry the potatoes thoroughly to achieve the crispiest frites and reduce oil splatter risk.
- Don't skimp on seasoning the steak; salt enhances the beef's flavor and helps form a desirable crust.

POSSIBLE VARIATIONS OF THE RECIPE

- **Herb Choice:** Experiment with different herb combinations in the butter, such as tarragon or chervil for a different flavor profile.
- **Sweet Potato Frites:** Use sweet potatoes instead of russet for a sweeter, healthier alternative rich in vitamins.
- **Sauce Variation:** Instead of garlic-herb butter, top your steak with a red wine reduction or a creamy peppercorn sauce for a different taste experience.

HEALTH NOTE & CALORIC INFORMATION

A standard serving of steak frites with garlic-herb butter can vary, but typically contains:

- Calories: approximately 750-900
- Protein: 45-55g
- Carbohydrates: 30-45g
- Fat: 50-65g
- Saturated Fat: 20-30g
- Fiber: 2-4g

Sodium: 500-1,000mg This can vary depending on the cut of meat, portion size, and specific ingredients used. The dish is high in protein and provides iron from the steak and vitamin C from the potatoes. However, it is also high in saturated fats and should be consumed in moderation.

CROQUE MONSIEUR

Hailing from French cafés and bistros in the early 1900s, the Croque Monsieur is a toasted sandwich that embodies the sophistication of French cuisine with simplicity and elegance. Its name translates to "mister crunch," a nod to its crispy exterior. Legend has it that French workers accidentally left their lunch of ham and cheese sandwiches near a hot radiator, and thus the concept of the toasted ham and cheese was born. It quickly become a quintessential quick meal in France.

INGREDIENTS

- 8 slices of good quality white bread
- 4 slices of tender cooked ham
- 2 cups of grated Gruyère cheese or a mix of Gruyère and Emmental
- 1 tablespoon of unsalted butter, more for spreading
- 1 tablespoon of all-purpose flour
- 1 cup of milk
- A pinch of nutmeg
- Salt and freshly ground black pepper, to taste
- 1 teaspoon of Dijon mustard
- Optional: 1/2 cup of finely grated Parmesan cheese for topping

DIRECTIONS

1. Start by making the béchamel sauce. In a small saucepan, melt 1 tablespoon of butter over medium heat. Once the butter is bubbling, add the flour and stir constantly for about 2 minutes to cook the flour without letting it brown.
2. Slowly whisk in the milk, ensuring that no lumps form. Continue to whisk and cook the mixture until it thickens into a smooth sauce, which should take about 5 minutes. Add nutmeg, a pinch of salt, and black pepper. Set aside to cool slightly.
3. Preheat your oven broiler to a medium setting.
4. Lightly butter one side of each slice of bread. On the unbuttered sides, spread a thin layer of Dijon mustard.
5. Build the sandwich by placing a slice of ham on the mustard-side of four bread slices. Cover the ham with a generous amount of grated Gruyère (or mix).
6. Place the other slice of bread on top, buttered side facing up, to make the sandwich.
7. In a large oven-safe frying pan over medium heat, fry the sandwiches until the bottom is golden brown, then flip and repeat on the other side.
8. Once both sides are toasted, transfer the sandwiches to a baking sheet. Spoon and spread the béchamel sauce on the top side of the sandwiches and sprinkle with more Gruyère and optional Parmesan.
9. Place the sandwiches under the broiler until the cheese is bubbling and starts to brown.
10. Serve the Croque Monsieurs immediately, cutting in half if desired.

DIETARY MODIFICATIONS

Gluten-Free: Use gluten-free bread and either make sure your all-purpose flour in the béchamel is gluten-free or substitute it with a gluten-free thickening agent like cornstarch.

Lactose Intolerance: Opt for lactose-free milk and lactose-free versions of Gruyère and Parmesan. Many hard, aged cheeses are naturally lower in lactose.

Vegetarian: Replace ham with layers of grilled vegetables like zucchini, eggplant, or roasted red peppers for a veggie-friendly alternative without losing the depth of flavor.

INGREDIENT SPOTLIGHT: GRUYÈRE CHEESE

Gruyère cheese, originating from the Swiss town of Gruyères, is a creamy, unpasteurized semi-hard cheese. The nuttiness and slight sweetness make Gruyère a perfect melting cheese, which is why it's the star in this sandwich's filling and topping. It's not just great for sandwiches—Gruyère is also a key ingredient in fondues, quiches, and the traditional French onion soup.

CHEF'S TIPS

- Use day-old bread as it holds up better under the weight of the béchamel and melted cheese.
- Shred your own cheese rather than buying pre-shredded, as it melts more uniformly and has a fresher taste.
- The béchamel should be thick enough to coat the back of a spoon; if too thick, stir in a bit more milk until you reach the desired consistency.
- While broiling, keep a close eye on the sandwiches, as the bread can go from perfectly toasted to burnt in a matter of seconds.
- For a richer béchamel sauce, add a pinch of grated aged cheese into the sauce while cooking.

POSSIBLE VARIATIONS OF THE RECIPE

- **Croque Madame:** Simply top each sandwich with a fried egg. The yolk adds a rich, creamy texture that contrasts beautifully with the crunch of the bread.
- **Croque Provençal:** Add a slice of tomato and some Provençal herbs on the ham before adding the cheese to bring a touch of the Mediterranean to the dish.
- **Croque Normand:** Substitute the ham for slices of cooked apple and replace Gruyère with Camembert for a sweet and savory Norman twist.

HEALTH NOTE & CALORIC INFORMATION

A traditional Croque Monsieur contains approximately 650-750 calories per sandwich, with the majority of calories coming from bread, cheese, and ham. It's high in protein and calcium but also high in sodium and saturated fat, so it's best enjoyed as an occasional indulgence rather than an everyday meal.

CLASSIC FRENCH TARTE TATIN

Tarte Tatin (pronounced taart ta-TAN) is a French upside-down apple tart named after the Tatin sisters who served it in their hotel, the Hôtel Tatin, in the late 1800s. According to culinary legend, it was accidentally created when Stéphanie Tatin was trying to make a traditional apple pie. In a hurry, she left the apples cooking in butter and sugar for too long. In an attempt to rescue the dessert, she covered the apples with a pastry top, baked it, and then inverted it to serve. The delightful result has secured the Tarte Tatin a place in the pantheon of French cuisine.

INGREDIENTS

- 1 sheet of puff pastry
- 6 large apples (preferably a mixture of sweet and tart varieties like Gala and Granny Smith)
- 100g (1/2 cup) unsalted butter
- 150g (3/4 cup) granulated sugar
- 1 tsp vanilla extract
- Pinch of salt
- Optional: whipped cream or vanilla ice cream for serving

DIRECTIONS

1. Preheat your oven to 190°C (375°F).
2. Peel, core, and cut the apples into quarters.
3. In an ovenproof skillet or a tarte tatin dish over medium heat, melt the butter, add the sugar, vanilla extract, and a pinch of salt, stirring until the sugar dissolves and the mixture starts to bubble.
4. Arrange the apple quarters in the skillet in a circular pattern with the rounded sides facing down. Cook the apples over medium heat for about 15 minutes, or until the butter-sugar mixture turns golden and the apples start to soften.
5. While the apples cook, roll out your puff pastry into a circle slightly larger than the top of the skillet.
6. Once the apples are caramelized, remove the skillet from the heat and lay the puff pastry over the apples, tucking the edges down around the sides of the apples.
7. Bake in the preheated oven for about 20-25 minutes, or until the puff pastry is puffed and golden brown.
8. Remove from the oven and let it cool for about 10 minutes. Carefully invert the tarte onto a plate by placing the plate on top of the skillet and flipping it in one quick motion.
9. Serve warm with a dollop of whipped cream or a scoop of vanilla ice cream.

DIETARY MODIFICATIONS

Gluten-Free: Substitute the traditional puff pastry with a gluten-free puff pastry available at specialty stores or make your own using gluten-free flour.

Lactose-Intolerant: Use a dairy-free butter substitute to cook the apples and check that your puff pastry does not contain any dairy ingredients.

Vegan: Use a dairy-free butter alternative and a vegan puff pastry, ensuring that all ingredients are free from animal products.

INGREDIENT SPOTLIGHT: PUFF PASTRY

Puff pastry is a light, flaky, unleavened pastry containing several layers of fat which is in solid state at 20°C (68°F). In raw form, it is a dough which is spread with solid fat and repeatedly folded and rolled out. The gaps that form between the layers left by the fat melting are pushed (leavened) by the water turning into steam during the baking process. Puff pastry's high butter content provides rich flavor and puffiness in baked goods, making it an ideal choice for Tarte Tatin, where it offers a delightful contrast to the caramelized apples.

CHEF'S TIPS

- Choose the right types of apples. A mix of sweet and tart varieties will give the tarte a balanced flavor.
- Caramelization is key. Cook the butter and sugar until it turns a deep amber color to get the signature caramel flavor.
- Don't skimp on the cooling time. Allowing the tarte to cool slightly helps the caramel set and prevents the tart from falling apart when inverted.
- Be careful when flipping the tarte. Use oven mitts and be confident in one fluid motion to avoid spills or breaks.
- If the pastry puffs up too much during baking, gently poke a few holes in it with a knife to release the steam.

POSSIBLE VARIATIONS OF THE RECIPE

- **Pear Tarte Tatin:** Switch out the apples for pears for a different, but still traditionally French, variation.
- **Savory Tarte Tatin:** Replace the apples with tomatoes, caramelized onions, and herbs to create a savory version. Omit the vanilla and serve as an appetizer or main course.
- **Tropical Tarte Tatin:** Give the dessert a tropical twist by using pineapples and a sprinkle of coconut flakes for the topping.

HEALTH NOTE & CALORIC INFORMATION

A slice of Tarte Tatin typically contains calories ranging from 300 to 400 depending on the size and the specific ingredients used. It is a rich source of carbohydrates and sugars due to the pastry and the caramelized fruit. It also contains fats from the butter and possibly a small amount of protein from the puff pastry. Serving it with whipped cream or ice cream increases the calorie and fat content.

CLASSIC SALADE NIÇOISE

Salade Niçoise hails from Nice, on the Mediterranean coast of France. Its creation is a palate portrait of the region, featuring ingredients that reflect the fresh, colorful, and diverse produce available in the Provence-Alpes-Côte d'Azur. Simultaneously simplistic and complex, this salad traditionally combines raw vegetables with boiled eggs, tinned fish, and anchovies, tied together with a zesty vinaigrette. It's a lovely play of textures and flavors that embodies the essence of French bistro cuisine.

INGREDIENTS

For the Salad:
- 200g fresh green beans, trimmed
- 4 small ripe tomatoes, wedged
- 1 small red onion, thinly sliced
- 1 bell pepper (preferably yellow or red), sliced
- 8 small new potatoes
- 4 eggs
- 1 head of Boston lettuce, leaves separated
- 1 can (150g) high-quality tuna in olive oil, drained
- 20 Niçoise or Kalamata olives
- 4 anchovy fillets (optional)
- Fresh basil leaves, for garnish

For the Vinaigrette:
- 60ml extra virgin olive oil
- 20ml red wine vinegar
- 1 tsp Dijon mustard
- 1 small garlic clove, minced
- Salt and freshly ground black pepper

DIRECTIONS

1. Start by boiling the potatoes in a pot of salted water until they are tender, which should take about 15 minutes. Once cooked, drain and set aside to cool slightly, then slice into halves or quarters depending on size.
2. While the potatoes are boiling, bring another pot of water to a boil and plunge in the green beans for about 4 minutes, until just tender but still crisp. Drain and immediately immerse them in ice water to stop the cooking process, ensuring they retain their vibrant color.
3. For the hard-boiled eggs, bring a pot of water to a boil, gently add the eggs, and cook for 9 minutes. Drain the eggs and place them in ice water to cool down before peeling and quartering them.
4. To assemble the salad, lay out the lettuce leaves on a large platter as a base. Arrange the green beans, potatoes, tomato wedges, red onion slices, and sliced bell pepper aesthetically on the bed of lettuce.
5. Next, flake the tuna and scatter it over the top of the vegetables, along with the olives and anchovies if using.
6. Prepare the vinaigrette by whisking together the olive oil, red wine vinegar, Dijon mustard, minced garlic, salt, and freshly ground black pepper until emulsified.
7. Drizzle the vinaigrette evenly over the assembled salad.
8. Finally, place the quartered eggs around the salad and garnish with fresh basil leaves before serving.

DIETARY MODIFICATIONS

Vegetarian: Omit the tuna and anchovies. To keep the protein content up, add chickpeas or white beans marinated in a bit of the vinaigrette.

Vegan: Follow the vegetarian substitutions and replace the boiled eggs with diced avocado for creaminess and additional nutrients.

Gluten-Free: This recipe is inherently gluten-free, but always check condiments such as Dijon mustard for any hidden gluten.

INGREDIENT SPOTLIGHT: EXTRA VIRGIN OLIVE OIL

Extra virgin olive oil is the star of Mediterranean cooking and is essential for the vinaigrette in this recipe. Made from pure, cold-pressed olives, this oil not only imparts a fruity, slightly peppery taste but also offers health benefits like antioxidants and heart-healthy monounsaturated fats. The history of olive oil dates back thousands of years, being a staple in diets and rituals across many cultures. For the best flavor and health benefits, choose a high-quality, extra virgin olive oil for your dressing.

CHEF'S TIPS

- Ensure all vegetables are dry before assembling to keep the salad from becoming soggy.
- Invest in a high-quality canned tuna, preferably one packed in olive oil, for the best flavor and texture.
- The key to a crisp green bean is the ice bath immediately after boiling – don't skip this step!
- Make the vinaigrette in a separate bowl and emulsify before dressing to evenly distribute the flavors.
- Garnish with fresh herbs like basil to add a burst of color and an extra layer of fresh flavor.

POSSIBLE VARIATIONS OF THE RECIPE

- **Grilled Version:** Grill the green beans, bell pepper, and fresh tuna steak (instead of canned tuna) for a smoky flavor.
- **Autumn Twist:** Roast the potatoes and butternut squash cubes to add warmth and a roasted flavor profile for cooler months.
- **Low-Carb Option:** Replace the potatoes with steamed or grilled zucchini slices and omit the beans for a lighter version of this salad.

HEALTH NOTE & CALORIC INFORMATION

A serving of Salade Niçoise is rich in fiber, vitamins (especially Vitamin C and A), and provides a good balance of carbohydrates, protein, and healthy fats from the ingredients like olive oil and fish. A typical serving (one-quarter of the recipe) contains roughly:

- Calories: 350-400
- Carbohydrates: 30g
- Protein: 20g
- Fat: 20g
- Fiber: 5g

CLASSIC FRENCH CASSOULET

The cassoulet is a heartwarming French dish, emblematic of the region of Languedoc. Originating in the city of Castelnaudary during the Hundred Years' War, this rich slow-cooked casserole bears peasant roots but has ascended to haute cuisine. Its name derives from the pot it's traditionally cooked in, the "cassole." There are debates over the 'authentic' recipe, with variations in Carcassonne and Toulouse, but the constants are white beans, meats, and a slow melding of deep flavors.

INGREDIENTS

- 1 lb dried white beans (Tarbais or cannellini)
- 8 cups water, for soaking the beans
- 1 onion, peeled and halved
- 2 cloves garlic, peeled and minced
- 1 large carrot, peeled and diced
- 2 stalks celery, diced
- 1 pound pork shoulder, cut into chunks
- ½ pound pancetta or bacon, chopped
- 1-pound confit duck legs (or a mix of duck and goose)
- 4 Toulouse sausages or other garlic pork sausages
- 1 cup chicken stock
- 1 can (14 oz) diced tomatoes
- 4 sprigs fresh thyme
- 2 bay leaves
- Salt and pepper to taste
- Breadcrumbs, for topping
- Fresh parsley, chopped for garnish

DIRECTIONS

1. The night before, place the beans in a large bowl and cover with water by at least 2 inches. Let soak overnight.
2. The next day, drain the beans and place them in a large pot. Cover with fresh water, add the halved onion, and bring to a boil. Lower the heat and simmer for about 45 minutes, until the beans are tender. Add salt towards the end of cooking. Drain, discarding the onion, and set aside.
3. Preheat oven to 325°F (165°C).
4. In a large Dutch oven or heavy-bottomed pot, brown the pancetta or bacon over medium heat until it renders its fat. Remove with a slotted spoon and set aside.
5. In the same pot, add the pork shoulder pieces and brown on all sides. Remove and set aside with the pancetta.
6. If needed, add a bit of oil to the pot, then add garlic, carrot, and celery. Cook until the vegetables begin to soften.
7. Return the pancetta and pork shoulder to the pot. Add the sausages and duck legs, nestling them into the mixture.
8. Pour in the chicken stock and diced tomatoes, then add the cooked white beans. Stir gently.
9. Add the thyme and bay leaves, then season with salt and pepper.
10. Cover the pot and transfer it to the preheated oven. Cook for 2 to 2½ hours, checking periodically to ensure it doesn't dry out—if it does, add a little more stock.
11. Uncover, sprinkle breadcrumbs over the top, and increase oven temperature to 375°F (190°C). Bake for another 40-50 minutes until the top is golden and crusty.
12. Let the cassoulet stand for 15 minutes before serving. Garnish with fresh parsley.

DIETARY MODIFICATIONS

Vegetarian: Substitute meats with a combination of vegetarian sausages, mushrooms, and smoked tofu to provide umami flavor. Be sure to enrich the dish with a robust vegetable stock.

Vegan: Follow the vegetarian suggestions, and also replace the breadcrumbs with a vegan alternative, or simply top with nutritional yeast for a cheese-like flavor before the final baking.

Gluten-Free: Ensure sausages are gluten-free and top the cassoulet with a gluten-free breadcrumb alternative or crispy fried onions for texture.

INGREDIENT SPOTLIGHT: TARBAIS BEANS

These white beans are the traditional choice for cassoulet and hail from Tarbes in southwest France. Tarbais beans are known for their thin skin and tender flesh which makes them particularly well-suited for absorbing flavors. These beans are grown in a manner that respects the "Label Rouge" quality standard, which ensures a high-quality product. The beans are key to a cassoulet as they provide not only substance but act as sponges, soaking up the rich, savoury flavors of the meats and stock during the slow cooking process.

CHEF'S TIPS
- Cook the beans just to tenderness—they should still hold their shape to avoid turning to mush during the long cook.
- Brown meats thoroughly before adding to the stew to develop depth of flavor.
- Resist the urge to stir the pot once it's in the oven; this can break down the beans and meats and disturb the developing crust.
- For a superior crust, consider sprinkling additional breadcrumbs and drizzling with duck fat halfway through the final baking phase.
- Use high-quality sausages and duck confit; their flavors are pillars in the ensemble of this rustic dish.

POSSIBLE VARIATIONS OF THE RECIPE
- **Quick Cassoulet:** Substitute the dried beans for canned to save on soaking time, and use store-bought duck confit.
- **Seafood Cassoulet:** Switch out traditional meats for firm fish, shrimp, and scallops, and use a seafood stock for a pescatarian take.
- **Summer Cassoulet:** Lighten the dish with chicken or turkey sausages, add a mixture of white and fresh fava beans, and include fresh tomatoes and basil.

HEALTH NOTE & CALORIC INFORMATION
A single serving of cassoulet can be quite calorie-dense due to the rich meats and slow-cooked beans. It can be estimated at around 600-800 calories per serving, with high protein content from the variety of meats and beans. It's also a good source of dietary fiber and iron but can be high in fat and sodium, so it should be enjoyed in moderation within a balanced diet.

PROVENÇAL BOUILLABAISSE

Bouillabaisse is more than just a traditional fish stew—it's a culinary legend from the port city of Marseille, France. The dish has humble beginnings, with origins dating back to when local fishermen would cook a stew using the bony rockfish they couldn't sell. Over time, it evolved into a beloved classic of French cuisine, celebrated for its rich flavor and aromatic broth. This bouillabaisse faithfully captures the essence of Provence, with each spoonful evoking the allure of the Mediterranean Sea.

INGREDIENTS

For the broth:
- 1/4 cup extra-virgin olive oil
- 2 onions, finely chopped
- 4 cloves of garlic, minced
- 3 ripe tomatoes, peeled and diced
- 1 fennel bulb, thinly sliced
- 2 leeks, white and light green parts only, cleaned and thinly sliced
- 1 teaspoon saffron threads
- 2 bay leaves
- 1 tablespoon fresh thyme leaves
- Zest of one orange
- 4 to 6 cups fish stock
- 1/2 cup white wine
- Salt and freshly ground pepper to taste

For the seafood:
- 2 pounds mixed firm fish fillets (such as red snapper, sea bass, halibut), cut into large chunks
- 1 pound shellfish (such as shrimp, mussels, or clams), cleaned
- 1/4 cup Pernod or pastis (optional)

To serve:
- Crusty bread
- Rouille sauce (optional)

DIRECTIONS

1. In a large pot or Dutch oven, heat the olive oil over medium heat. Add the onions and garlic, and sauté until they are soft but not browned, about 5 minutes.
2. Stir in the tomatoes, fennel, and leeks. Sauté for another 5-7 minutes until the vegetables are softened.
3. Add the saffron, bay leaves, thyme, and orange zest, stirring until the saffron begins to dissolve and the mixture is fragrant, about 1 minute.
4. Pour in the fish stock and white wine, then season with salt and pepper. Bring the mixture to a low simmer, and let it cook, partially covered, for about 20-25 minutes.
5. While the broth simmers, prepare the seafood. Make sure that the fish fillets are deboned and the shellfish are cleaned.
6. After the broth has simmered, add the fish chunks to the pot, and cook for about 5 minutes.
7. If using shellfish, add them to the pot now (discard any clams or mussels that haven't opened after cooking). If adding Pernod or pastis, pour it in at this point and cook for another 2-3 minutes.
8. Check the seasoning and adjust if necessary. Ladle the bouillabaisse into bowls, making sure there are pieces of fish and shellfish in each serving.
9. Serve hot with crusty bread on the side. If desired, offer rouille sauce to spread on the bread or stir into the stew.

DIETARY MODIFICATIONS

Vegetarian: Replace the fish and shellfish with hearty chunks of potatoes, artichokes, and large white beans. Use vegetable stock instead of fish stock, and consider adding a splash of liquid smoke to impart a deeper flavor reminiscent of the sea.

Vegan: Follow the vegetarian suggestions and ensure that the wine used is vegan (some wines use animal products in the filtering process). Skip the rouille sauce, or make a vegan version using silken tofu as a base blended with garlic, saffron, and olive oil.

Lactose Intolerance: The traditional Bouillabaisse recipe does not include lactose-containing ingredients. However, if serving with rouille sauce, make it with lactose-free mayonnaise or for a completely lactose-free dish, simply omit the rouille.

INGREDIENT SPOTLIGHT: SAFFRON

Saffron, the golden-hued spice heralded as the most expensive spice by weight, is derived from the dried stigmas of the saffron crocus (Crocus sativus). Historically prized for its color, flavor, and medicinal properties, saffron originated in Greece but spread across Eurasia, where it became a staple in various cuisines. In bouillabaisse, saffron imparts a distinctive earthy aroma and a vibrant color, playing a pivotal role in creating the stew's characteristic profile and becoming integral to its identity.

CHEF'S TIPS

- To extract maximum flavor from saffron, crush the threads slightly with a mortar and pestle and steep them in a bit of warm broth or water before adding to the pot.
- Source the freshest seafood possible, and ask your fishmonger for recommendations on what's in season for the best taste.
- The broth can be made in advance and refrigerated for up to two days, which allows the flavors to meld and deepen.
- Always taste and adjust the seasoning throughout the cooking process, as the broth concentrates and the ingredients release their flavors.
- Add the delicate seafood right at the end of cooking to avoid overcooking, which can result in a rubbery texture.

POSSIBLE VARIATIONS OF THE RECIPE

- Asian Twist Bouillabaisse: Introduce lemongrass, ginger, and a splash of coconut milk to the broth. Instead of traditional fish, use a mix of seafood commonly found in Asian cuisines like squid and scallops.
- Italian Cioppino Influence: Include a variety of Mediterranean herbs like oregano and basil, and use a generous pour of red wine instead of white. Add Italian sausage slices for an extra layer of flavor.
- Caribbean Flair: Incorporate coconut milk, allspice berries, and a Scotch bonnet pepper into the broth. Replace the traditional fish with red snapper and conch for authentic island taste.

HEALTH NOTE & CALORIC INFORMATION

A serving of Bouillabaisse is rich in protein and omega-3 fatty acids, thanks to the variety of seafood. The tomatoes, fennel, and leeks contribute vitamins, antioxidants, and fiber. A typical serving contains roughly 300-450 calories, but this can vary depending on the specific types of seafood and portions used. It is also relatively low in carbohydrates and may be suitable for low-carb diets if served without bread.

CONFIT DE CANARD
(DUCK CONFIT)

Originating from the Gascony region in France, Duck Confit is a classic French dish known for its rich flavor and tender texture. The word "confit" refers to the method of slowly cooking meat in its own fat, a preservation technique dating back to medieval times. This method not only imbued the duck with incredible flavor but also allowed it to be stored for months on end. Duck Confit has since become a gourmet delicacy, often served with potatoes and garlic to showcase its succulence.

INGREDIENTS

- 4 whole duck legs (thigh and drumstick)
- 4 tablespoons of kosher salt
- 4 cloves of garlic, minced
- 2 tablespoons of chopped fresh thyme
- 1 teaspoon of freshly ground black pepper
- 4 bay leaves
- 2 tablespoons of duck fat or olive oil
- Approximately 4 cups of rendered duck fat (may need more or less depending on the size of your cooking vessel)

DIRECTIONS

1. Rub the duck legs evenly with kosher salt, minced garlic, fresh thyme, and black pepper. Place bay leaves on the flesh side of the legs.
2. Lay the duck legs, skin side up, in a shallow dish, and cover with plastic wrap. Refrigerate for 24-36 hours to cure.
3. Preheat your oven to 275°F (135°C).
4. Remove the duck legs from the refrigerator and brush off the majority of the seasoning, but do not rinse.
5. In a Dutch oven or an ovenproof pot, arrange the duck legs skin side down and pour enough rendered duck fat over the duck legs to fully submerge them.
6. Transfer the pot to the preheated oven and cook for 2 to 3 hours, or until the meat is very tender and can be easily pierced with a knife.
7. Carefully remove the pot from the oven and let the duck legs cool in the fat. Once cool, you can store the duck legs in the fat in a sealed container in the refrigerator for up to several weeks.
8. When ready to serve, remove the duck legs from the fat and brush off excess. Heat 2 tablespoons of duck fat or olive oil in a large skillet over medium-high heat.
9. Place the duck legs skin side down in the skillet and cook until the skin is crisp, about 5-10 minutes.
10. Serve immediately, traditionally with garlicky potatoes and a side of salad.

DIETARY MODIFICATIONS

Vegetarian: This dish relies on duck, and there isn't a direct vegetarian substitute that will replicate the texture and flavor profile of duck. However, for a vegetarian take on luxurious, slow-cooked food, try confit tomatoes. Substitute duck for tomatoes, bake them in olive oil with garlic and herbs, and serve with crusty bread.

Vegan: Following from the vegetarian suggestion, vegan confit tomatoes can be seasoned with salt, thyme, and black pepper, then slow-baked in olive oil. Use the tomatoes to top a hearty bean stew for a satisfying meal, mimicking the richness of traditional confit.

Lactose Intolerance: Duck confit is inherently lactose-free, so no modifications are required.

INGREDIENT SPOTLIGHT: DUCK FAT

Duck fat is our spotlight ingredient. This culinary gold has been used in traditional French cooking for centuries. With a melting point lower than butter, it brings a delicate, silky texture to dishes and has a rich, yet subtle flavor that enhances the taste of anything cooked with it. The use of duck fat in this recipe is key not only for the confit technique itself but also for achieving the characteristic crisp skin and tender meat of a properly made Confit de Canard.

CHEF'S TIPS

- Quality of Duck Fat: Use high-quality, pure rendered duck fat for the best flavor and consistency in your confit.
- Curing Time: Do not shorten the curing time - the salt not only flavors the meat but also contributes to the unique texture of the confit.
- Oven Temperature: Ensure your oven temperature is accurate for even, slow cooking. Too high, and the meat will dry; too low, and it won't confit properly.
- Storage: If stored correctly, submerged in fat in an airtight container in the refrigerator, duck confit can last for a few months.
- Crisping the Skin: Be patient when crisping the skin in the skillet. Resist the urge to move the legs too much so that the skin has ample time to become golden and crisp.

POSSIBLE VARIATIONS OF THE RECIPE

- **Confit de Poulet:** Substitute chicken legs for duck for a milder flavor and a lower-cost alternative.
- **Aromatic Variations:** Try additional aromatics during the curing stage, such as orange zest or star anise, for a different flavor twist.
- **Confit de Porc:** Pork belly can be a rich and indulgent substitute for duck following the same confit technique, providing a different but equally savory experience.

HEALTH NOTE & CALORIC INFORMATION

Duck confit is high in protein and fat, with a moderate amount of calories.

One serving (a single duck leg) usually contains about 400-500 calories, depending on the size of the leg and the amount of fat absorbed.

While duck fat is praised for its taste, it is also rich in monounsaturated and polyunsaturated fats, which can be more beneficial to heart health compared to saturated fats.

CHOUCROUTE GARNIE À L'ALSACIENNE

Choucroute Garnie, hailing from the Alsace region of France, is a hearty dish that has warmed the hearts and bellies of the Alsatian people for centuries. Alsace, with its history of German and French influence, has created a melting pot of flavors that materialize in this iconic sauerkraut stew. Traditionally served in the colder months, Choucroute Garnie reflects the region's love for charcuterie and sauerkraut, with a French finesse in its preparation and presentation.

INGREDIENTS

- 1 kg sauerkraut, rinsed and drained
- 800 g of assorted smoked and fresh sausages (e.g., frankfurters, bratwurst, montbéliard)
- 300 g bacon, diced
- 400 g pork shoulder or loin, cut into large chunks
- 4 pork knuckles (optional)
- 1 large onion, chopped
- 4 cloves of garlic, minced
- 10 juniper berries
- 3 cloves
- 10 black peppercorns
- 1 bay leaf
- 750 ml dry white wine (Alsatian Riesling)
- 2 tbsp goose fat or oil
- 500 ml chicken or beef stock
- Potatoes for serving
- Fresh parsley for garnish
- Salt and pepper, to taste

DIRECTIONS

1. Start by rinsing the sauerkraut under cold water to remove some of the brine. Squeeze out excess water and set aside.
2. In a large Dutch oven or heavy-bottomed pot, heat the goose fat or oil over medium heat. Add the bacon and cook until it starts to brown.
3. Stir in the chopped onion and garlic, cooking until the onion is translucent. Add the juniper berries, cloves, peppercorns, and bay leaf. Cook for another minute to release the flavors.
4. Add the pork shoulder chunks and pork knuckles if using, browning them lightly on all sides.
5. Place the sauerkraut on top of the meats in the pot. Pour the white wine and stock over the sauerkraut. Bring to a simmer, then reduce the heat to low, cover, and let it cook gently for 1.5 to 2 hours, stirring occasionally.
6. In the meantime, if you're serving potatoes, boil or steam them until tender, and set aside.
7. After the sauerkraut mixture has cooked, nestle the sausages into the pot, ensuring they are submerged in the liquid. Cook for another 30 minutes or until the sausages are heated through.
8. Taste and adjust seasoning with salt and pepper. Be mindful of the sauerkraut and bacon's saltiness when adding additional salt.
9. To serve, remove the bay leaf and other whole spices if desired. Arrange the meats and sauerkraut on a large platter, along with the potatoes. Garnish with fresh parsley.

DIETARY MODIFICATIONS

Vegetarian: Replace meats with smoked tofu, tempeh, and a variety of mushrooms for umami. Use vegetable stock instead of chicken or beef stock. Ensure richness by using plenty of aromatic herbs and spices.

Vegan: Follow the vegetarian suggestions, and also ensure that the wine used is vegan-friendly. Instead of goose fat, use a high-smoked point plant oil like grapeseed oil.

Gluten-Free: Choucroute Garnie is naturally gluten-free, but always make sure that the sausages, stock, and other processed ingredients are certified gluten-free to avoid cross-contamination.

INGREDIENT SPOTLIGHT: ALSATIAN RIESLING

The spotlight ingredient in this recipe is Alsatian Riesling. This dry white wine is key to Choucroute Garnie as it imparts a crisp acidity and fruity undertone which balances out the richness of the meats and the tang of the sauerkraut. Alsatian Rieslings are typically fuller-bodied and more aromatic compared to their German counterparts, making them a perfect cooking wine for robust dishes such as this. (60 words)

CHEF'S TIPS

- Quality of sauerkraut: Opt for artisanal or homemade sauerkraut if possible—it's less acidic and has a better texture.
- Choice of meat: Use a variety of meats for different textures and flavors. Smoked meats provide depth while fresh sausages add a delicate contrast.
- Sausage timing: Adding sausages later in the cooking process prevents them from overcooking and maintains their texture.
- Wine selection: Choose a dry Alsatian Riesling for authenticity, avoid sweeter variants that could overshadow the savory profile of the dish.
- Serving suggestion: Serve with mustard and crusty bread for a complete Alsatian experience.

POSSIBLE VARIATIONS OF THE RECIPE

- **Beer Choucroute:** Substitute the white wine with a good lager or ale for a different flavor profile, catering to beer aficionados.
- **Fish Choucroute:** Replace meats with firm white fish, salmon, and prawns for a pescatarian twist on this Alsatian classic.
- **Fall Harvest Choucroute:** Incorporate apples and sweet potatoes into the sauerkraut mix for a sweet-and-sour take that celebrates autumn's bounty.

HEALTH NOTE & CALORIC INFORMATION

A standard serving of Choucroute Garnie contains approximately 600-800 calories, though this number may vary depending on the specific types and quantities of meat used. It is a high-protein, high-fat dish, with nutrients contributed by the sauerkraut such as vitamin C and probiotics. It's also relatively high in sodium, so it might not be suitable for those on a low-salt diet.

CLASSIC FRENCH TARTIFLETTE

Nestled in the Alps of France's Haute-Savoie region, the Tartiflette is a robust and hearty dish that was created to nourish the soul after a strenuous day. Though it is said to have been developed in the 1980s to promote sales of Reblochon cheese, its roots draw from a traditional recipe called "péla": a simple, gratin-like dish of potatoes, onions, and cheese. Tartiflette beautifully merges rustic charm with the opulence of creamy cheese, a meal that turns humble ingredients into a rich tapestry of flavor.

INGREDIENTS

- 1 kg (about 2.2 lbs) waxy potatoes, peeled
- 250 g (about 8.8 oz) smoked bacon lardons
- 2 medium onions, thinly sliced
- 3 cloves of garlic, minced
- 150 ml (about 5 fl oz) dry white wine
- 1 Reblochon cheese (about 450 g or 1 lb), chilled
- Salt and pepper, to taste
- 30 ml (2 tablespoons) olive oil or butter
- Handful of chopped fresh parsley (optional, for garnish)

DIRECTIONS

1. Preheat your oven to 200°C (approximately 390°F).
2. Place the peeled potatoes in a large pot, cover with cold water, and bring to a boil. Add a pinch of salt, then reduce heat and simmer until just tender but not falling apart, about 10-15 minutes. Drain and let cool slightly before slicing into 1/4 inch (0.5 cm) slices.
3. In a large frying pan, heat olive oil or butter over medium heat. Add the bacon lardons and cook until they start to crisp, about 5 minutes.
4. Add the sliced onions and cook with the lardons, stirring occasionally, until the onions are soft and golden, about 10 minutes.
5. Stir in the minced garlic and cook for an additional 1-2 minutes until fragrant.
6. Pour over the white wine and let the mixture cook until the wine has reduced by about half, which should take around 3-5 minutes.
7. In a large gratin dish, layer half of the sliced potatoes. Season with salt and pepper. Spread half of the lardon-onion mixture over the potatoes. Repeat with another layer of potatoes, and the rest of the lardon-onion mixture.
8. Cut the chilled Reblochon cheese horizontally to create two rounds. Place the cheese, skin-side up, on top of the onion and potato mixture.
9. Bake in the preheated oven for about 20-25 minutes, or until the cheese is bubbly and browned on top.
10. Remove from the oven, let it stand for 5 minutes, and garnish with parsley if desired before serving.

DIETARY MODIFICATIONS

Vegetarian: Replace the bacon lardons with a vegetarian bacon substitute or diced smoked tofu to retain some of the smoky flavor. You may also add a teaspoon of smoked paprika for added depth.

Vegan: In addition to the vegetarian bacon alternative, replace the Reblochon cheese with a dairy-free cheese that melts well. Nutritional yeast can be sprinkled in the layers for an added cheesy flavor.

Lactose Intolerance: Use a lactose-free cheese similar in texture to Reblochon, or a hard cheese like Gruyère. Be sure to confirm that the cheese used is lactose-free as some aged cheeses naturally have very little lactose.

INGREDIENT SPOTLIGHT: REBLOCHON CHEESE

Reblochon cheese is the heart of Tartiflette. This soft washed-rind and smear-ripened cheese hails from the Haute-Savoie region of France. "Reblocher" means "to pinch a cow's udder again," referring to the practice of holding back some of the milk from the first milking. This milk is much richer and is used to make Reblochon. The cheese has a fine velvety rind and a creamy center, with nutty flavors that are skyrocked when melted, making it integral for the authenticity of the dish.

CHEF'S TIPS

- For best texture, don't overcook the potatoes when boiling, as they will continue to cook in the oven.
- To enhance the flavors, allow the wine to reduce and concentrate the onion and bacon mixture's bite.
- The quality of the Reblochon cheese used is paramount. Look for a cheese with a soft, almost runny texture and an edible rind.
- Letting the Tartiflette stand after baking not only allows it to cool slightly, making it easier to serve, it also lets flavors meld.
- Should you be unable to find Reblochon, a mix of Brie and a stronger soft cheese like Munster can work as a substitute.

POSSIBLE VARIATIONS OF THE RECIPE

- **Lightened Up:** For a lighter version, substitute half of the potatoes with sliced leeks or zucchini and use a cheese lower in fat like Cantal.
- **Meat-Free Gourmet:** Layer in wild mushrooms sautéed with thyme and garlic to bring a luxurious and earthy flavor to the dish.
- **Spicy Tartiflette:** Add a diced jalapeño or a dash of cayenne pepper to the lardon-onion mix for those who crave a kick of heat.

HEALTH NOTE & CALORIC INFORMATION

A traditional Tartiflette is a rich dish, high in calories, fats, and carbs primarily due to the cheese and potatoes. A single serving can range from 600-800 calories, with substantial amounts of saturated fats from the cheese and bacon. However, it also provides protein and is a good source of energy. For those tracking their intake, moderation is key, and pairing with a green salad can balance the richness.

CŒUR DE FILET PROVENÇAL (PROVENÇAL HEART OF BEEF TENDERLOIN)

Cœur de Filet Provençal takes its inspiration from the rustic yet refined flavors of Provence, a region in the South of France known for its aromatic herbs, garlic, and olive oil. This dish is a celebration of simple ingredients that come together to create an elegant and flavorful entrée, perfect for impressing at a dinner party or a romantic evening at home.

INGREDIENTS

- 2 beef tenderloin steaks, each about 6 oz (170 g)
- 2 Tbsp extra-virgin olive oil
- 2 cloves garlic, minced
- 1 tsp fresh rosemary, finely chopped
- 1 tsp fresh thyme leaves
- 1/2 tsp dried lavender (optional)
- Salt and freshly ground black pepper, to taste
- 1/4 cup dry white wine
- 1/2 cup cherry tomatoes, halved
- 1/4 cup Kalamata olives, pitted and halved
- 1/4 cup red bell pepper, diced
- 2 Tbsp capers, drained
- 1 Tbsp fresh parsley, chopped for garnish

DIRECTIONS

1. Take the beef tenderloin steaks out of the refrigerator and allow them to come to room temperature, about 30 minutes before cooking.
2. Preheat a heavy skillet over medium-high heat and add the olive oil.
3. Season the steaks with salt, black pepper, minced garlic, rosemary, thyme, and dried lavender (if using), ensuring they are well-coated.
4. Once the skillet is hot, place the steaks in the skillet. Cook for about 4 minutes on each side for medium-rare, or until they reach your desired level of doneness. Use a meat thermometer to check for accuracy—135°F for medium-rare.
5. Remove the steaks from the skillet and let them rest on a plate, covered with foil.
6. In the same skillet over medium heat, add the white wine and scrape the bottom to deglaze, picking up any browned bits from the steak.
7. Add the cherry tomatoes, Kalamata olives, red bell pepper, and capers to the skillet. Cook for about 3-4 minutes until the tomatoes start to soften.
8. Taste and adjust the seasoning of the sauce if necessary.
9. Place the steaks on serving plates and spoon the Provençal vegetable mixture over them.
10. Garnish with fresh parsley and serve immediately.

DIETARY MODIFICATIONS

Vegetarian: Swap out the beef tenderloin for thick slices of eggplant or portobello mushroom caps. Follow the same seasoning and cooking instructions, and be careful not overcook, as these vegetables don't require as much time as beef.

Vegan: In addition to the vegetarian substitution, replace the white wine with vegetable broth to ensure the deglazing liquid is vegan-friendly.

Lactose Intolerance: The recipe does not contain lactose products, so it is suitable as is for those with lactose intolerance.

INGREDIENT SPOTLIGHT: DRIED LAVENDER

Dried lavender adds a unique floral note that is not common in many cuisines but is a signature in Provençal cooking. It is distinctive for its fresh, sweet aroma that pairs excellently with hearty dishes. Lavender has been used for centuries in Provence, both for its scent and for its culinary applications. When using lavender in cooking, it's important to use a culinary-grade product and to do so sparingly, as its strong flavor can become overpowering.

CHEF'S TIPS

- Pat dry the beef tenderloin steaks before seasoning to ensure a nice sear and prevent steaming.
- Allow the steaks to rest after cooking to redistribute the juices and ensure a tender, juicy steak.
- Use quality extra-virgin olive oil for the best flavor, as it's a significant ingredient in Provençal cuisine.
- Be cautious with lavender; it can quickly dominate the dish, so less is often more.
- Cook the Provençal vegetable mixture until just tender to maintain some texture and freshness.

POSSIBLE VARIATIONS OF THE RECIPE

- **Red Wine Reduction:** Instead of white wine, use a red wine for the deglazing liquid and reduce it to a syrupy consistency for a richer sauce.
- **Herb-Crusted Steak:** Mix breadcrumbs with finely chopped herbs and coat the oiled steaks before searing to create a crispy, flavorful crust.
- **Mediterranean Relish:** Add diced cucumber, a splash of lemon juice, and feta cheese crumbles to the vegetable mixture for a refreshing Mediterranean twist.

HEALTH NOTE & CALORIC INFORMATION

This dish is a high-protein, low-carb meal. It's rich in monounsaturated fats from the olive oil and provides a range of vitamins and antioxidants from the herbs and vegetables. Each serving of Cœur de Filet Provençal (without modifications) is approximately 390 calories, with 25 grams of fat, 35 grams of protein, and 4 grams of carbohydrates.

GRATIN DAUPHINOIS (FRENCH POTATO GRATIN)

Originating from the Dauphiné region in southeastern France, Gratin Dauphinois is a classic French dish that epitomizes the art of comfort food. This traditional recipe dates back to the 17th century and was served at the dinner table of the French nobility. It showcases the humble potato in a rich, creamy backdrop, adorned with a golden crust of cheese. Ideal for cozier nights or as a sophisticated side, this dish captures simplicity and elegance on a plate.

INGREDIENTS

- 2 lbs (about 900g) of starchy potatoes, peeled and thinly sliced
- 2 cloves of garlic, minced
- 1 cup (240 ml) of heavy cream
- 1 cup (240 ml) of whole milk
- Salt to taste
- Freshly ground black pepper to taste
- A pinch of freshly grated nutmeg
- 4 ounces (about 115g) of Gruyère cheese, grated
- 2 tablespoons of unsalted butter
- Fresh thyme leaves, for garnish (optional)

DIRECTIONS

1. Preheat your oven to 350°F (175°C).
2. Rub a baking dish with a halved garlic clove and then butter the dish generously.
3. In a saucepan, combine the heavy cream, milk, minced garlic, salt, pepper, and nutmeg. Bring the mixture to a simmer over medium heat.
4. Add the sliced potatoes to the saucepan and ensure they are evenly coated with the mixture. Simmer for about 10 minutes, stirring occasionally, until the potatoes start to become tender.
5. Transfer half of the potatoes using a slotted spoon to the prepared baking dish, spreading them out evenly.
6. Sprinkle half of the grated Gruyère cheese over the potatoes.
7. Add the remaining potatoes to the dish, and then pour over the remaining cream mixture from the saucepan.
8. Top with the rest of the Gruyère cheese and dot the surface with small pieces of butter.
9. Bake in the preheated oven for about 1 hour, or until the top is golden browned and bubbling, and the potatoes are completely tender.
10. Let the gratin cool for at least 10 minutes before serving. This allows the layers to set slightly and the flavors to meld. Garnish with fresh thyme leaves if desired.

DIETARY MODIFICATIONS

Vegetarian: The traditional Gratin Dauphinois is already vegetarian. Ensure that the cheese used is made without animal rennet to be fully vegetarian-friendly.

Vegan: Substitute the dairy products with plant-based alternatives. Use a rich coconut cream and unsweetened almond milk for the creamy base and a vegan cheese alternative for the Gruyère. Earthy, aged vegan cheeses work well for mimicking the depth of flavor.

Lactose Intolerance: Use lactose-free versions of cream and milk and a lactose-free cheese, or a hard-aged cheese like traditional Gruyère, which has a very low lactose content that is usually tolerable for those with lactose intolerance.

INGREDIENT SPOTLIGHT: GRUYÈRE CHEESE

Gruyère cheese is known for its rich, creamy, slightly nutty flavor and excellent melting properties. It is named after the Swiss town of Gruyères and has been produced since the 12th century. A good Gratin Dauphinois hinges on the quality of the Gruyère; its ability to form a luscious, bubbly crust without becoming oily is why it's the preferred choice. Authentic Swiss Gruyère carries a designated AOC (Appellation d'Origine Contrôlée) status, confirming its traditional production methods and regional origin.

CHEF'S TIPS

- Slice the potatoes very thinly to ensure they cook through and absorb the creamy sauce; a mandoline slicer can provide even slices quickly.
- Do not rinse the potatoes after slicing; the starch helps thicken the sauce.
- Slowly simmer the cream mixture with potatoes to infuse the flavor and pre-cook the potatoes, which leads to a more delicate texture in the final dish.
- Allow the dish to rest before serving to let flavors combine and the cream set slightly for easier serving.
- If you prefer a more pronounced garlic flavor, add an extra minced clove to the cream mixture.

POSSIBLE VARIATIONS OF THE RECIPE

- **Herb-Infused:** Before baking, infuse the cream with a bay leaf, fresh rosemary, or other preferred herbs for an aromatic twist.
- **Cheese Twist:** Experiment with other melting cheeses like Emmental, sharp Cheddar, or Comté for a different flavor profile.
- **Bacon-Laced:** For a non-vegetarian variant, layer crispy cooked bacon between the potato layers before baking for a smoky crunch.

HEALTH NOTE & CALORIC INFORMATION

Gratin Dauphinois is rich in calories due to the heavy cream and cheese. A serving typically contains around 300-400 calories, with a considerable amount of fat, mostly saturated, from the dairy products. It also provides carbohydrates from the potatoes and protein from the cheese. To create a lighter version, use half-and-half instead of heavy cream, and reduce the amount of cheese.

BOUDIN NOIR AUX POMMES
(BLOOD SAUSAGE WITH APPLES)

A rustic French dish that dates back to the time when every part of the pig was used after slaughter. Boudin Noir, or blood sausage, is a rich and flavorful component traditionally paired with something sweet and tart, like apples, to balance its intense flavor. This dish is commonly enjoyed in the cooler months and is a testament to the tradition of nose-to-tail eating, showcasing French culinary finesse in transforming simple ingredients into gourmet fare.

INGREDIENTS

- 4 boudin noir sausages (blood sausages)
- 4 large apples, varieties such as Granny Smith or Braeburn
- 2 tablespoons unsalted butter
- 2 tablespoons brown sugar
- 1/2 cup apple cider
- Salt and black pepper, to taste
- Fresh parsley, chopped (for garnish)

DIRECTIONS

1. Begin by gently pricking the boudin noir sausages with a fork. This will prevent them from bursting during cooking.
2. Heat a non-stick frying pan over medium heat and cook the sausages for about 10-15 minutes, turning occasionally, until they are heated through and slightly crisp on the outside. Make sure not to cook them on too high heat as they can burst.
3. While the sausages cook, peel, core, and slice the apples into wedges.
4. In another pan, melt the butter over medium heat. Add the apple slices and sprinkle them with brown sugar, stirring to coat.
5. Cook the apples until they begin to soften, which will take about 5-7 minutes.
6. Pour the apple cider over the apples, and season with a pinch of salt and black pepper. Continue to cook, frequently stirring until the cider has reduced and formed a syrupy glaze over the apples, for about 10 minutes.
7. To serve, place the boudin noir on a warm plate with the caramelized apples around it. Drizzle any remaining glaze from the apples over the sausages.
8. Garnish with fresh chopped parsley and serve immediately.

DIETARY MODIFICATIONS

Vegetarian: Use a vegetarian sausage alternative that has a rich, umami flavor, such as smoked tofu sausages. Ensure they have a robust texture to stand up to pan-frying.

Vegan: Similar to the vegetarian option, but also substitute the butter with a vegan alternative like coconut oil, which will add a subtle complementary flavor to the apples.

Lactose Intolerance: Simply use lactose-free butter or a lactose-free butter alternative like clarified butter (ghee), which will fry the apples to caramelized perfection without the lactose.

INGREDIENT SPOTLIGHT: BOUDIN NOIR

Boudin Noir is a type of blood sausage that originated in Europe. It's made with pork blood, fat, and fillers such as onions, bread, and seasonings. Despite its potentially polarizing main ingredient, boudin noir is a beloved component of traditional French cuisine. The rich, earthy flavors are balanced by cooking techniques and complementary sides like tart apples. Its presence in this dish offers a culinary adventure into the depth of flavors and history.

CHEF'S TIPS

- For optimal texture, allow the sausages to come to room temperature before cooking them.
- Be delicate when pricking the sausages; too deep and they can fall apart during cooking.
- Use a thick-bottomed pan to prevent the apples from burning as they caramelize.
- If the glaze reduces too quickly, add a bit more apple cider, a tablespoon at a time.
- To add complexity, a splash of Calvados (apple brandy) can be added with the apple cider for further enhancement of the apple flavor.

POSSIBLE VARIATIONS OF THE RECIPE

- **With a twist of spices:** Add a pinch of cinnamon and nutmeg to the apples while they caramelize for a warm spice note.
- **Savory-Sweet:** Incorporate sautéed onions with the apples and finish with a balsamic vinegar reduction for a savory-sweet balance.
- **Pear substitution:** For a sweeter and more delicate fruit component, replace apples with pears following the same cooking process.

HEALTH NOTE & CALORIC INFORMATION

This dish provides a good source of protein from the boudin noir but is quite rich in fat due to the nature of the sausage and added butter. The apples offer dietary fiber and vitamin C. Portions should be accounted for accordingly, as boudin noir is calorically dense. A typical serving of this dish is high in cholesterol and sodium, and guests with dietary restrictions related to these should consume it in moderation. Nutritional content can vary considerably based on sausage preparation and size; however, an average portion size could approximate 600 to 800 calories.

CHARME DE CHABLIS:
ANDOUILLETTE WITH MUSTARD CREAM SAUCE

Originating from France, andouillette is a distinctive sausage made primarily from the intestines and stomach of the pig. Its history can be traced back to the Middle Ages when offal was a common staple of European diets due to its affordability. In particular, andouillette is a specialty of the Troyes region in Champagne, but it has enamored tastebuds across France and beyond. This version -- bathed in a mustard cream sauce -- is aptly named "Charme de Chablis" for the wine that compliments it and the captivating flavor it offers.

INGREDIENTS

- 4 andouillette sausages
- 1 tablespoon vegetable oil
- 2 shallots, finely chopped
- 1 clove garlic, minced
- 1/2 cup Chablis or a similar dry white wine
- 1 cup heavy cream
- 2 tablespoons Dijon mustard
- 1 tablespoon whole grain mustard
- Salt and pepper to taste
- Chopped parsley for garnish
- Crusty French bread for serving

DIRECTIONS

1. Begin by preheating your oven to 350°F (175°C).
2. Heat the vegetable oil in a large oven-proof skillet over medium-high heat.
3. Gently add the andouillette sausages to the skillet and sear them until they are browned on all sides, approximately 3 minutes per side.
4. Remove the sausages and set them aside. In the same skillet, reduce the heat to medium and add the chopped shallots, cooking until soft and translucent, around 2 minutes.
5. Stir in the minced garlic and cook for another 30 seconds, until fragrant.
6. Pour in the Chablis, scraping up any browned bits from the bottom of the skillet. Allow the wine to reduce by half, which will take about 3-4 minutes.
7. Lower the heat to a simmer and mix in the heavy cream, Dijon mustard, and whole grain mustard. Season the sauce with salt and pepper to taste.
8. Return the sausages to the skillet and spoon the sauce over them.
9. Transfer the skillet to the preheated oven and bake for 10-15 minutes, or until the andouillettes are cooked through and the sauce has thickened slightly.
10. Garnish with chopped parsley and serve hot with crusty French bread.

DIETARY MODIFICATIONS

Gluten-free: Substitute the French bread with a gluten-free variety. Ensure the mustards used do not contain any gluten additives.

Dairy-free: Replace the heavy cream with a dairy-free alternative such as coconut cream or a soy-based cream. Adjust the quantity if necessary to achieve the right sauce consistency.

Low-Fat Alternative: For a low-fat version, use reduced-fat cream or a blend of milk and cornstarch as a thickener. Opt for whole grain mustard that's lower in calories, and serve with whole-grain bread.

INGREDIENT SPOTLIGHT: DIJON MUSTARD

Dijon mustard originated in the city of Dijon, the capital of Burgundy, France. Known for its pale, yellowish hue and creamy consistency, it is sharper than yellow mustard but less spicy than English mustard. Its flavor is owed to the use of brown mustard seeds and white wine or a mix of vinegar and water. Dijon mustard adds depth and piquancy to countless recipes and is indispensable in this dish, providing a pronounced but smooth heat that perfectly complements the richness of the andouillette.

CHEF'S TIPS
- Handle with Care: When searing the andouillette, turn them gently to avoid breaking the casing.
- Optimize for Flavor: Use a good quality dry white wine that you would enjoy drinking. The wine adds a significant layer of flavor to the sauce.
- Consistency is Key: After adding the cream, consistently stir to ensure the sauce does not split or curdle.
- Mind the Mustard: Balance the two types of mustard to taste, depending on how sharp or mellow you like the sauce.
- Rest & Serve: Let the sausages rest for a couple of minutes before serving to allow the juices to redistribute.

POSSIBLE VARIATIONS OF THE RECIPE
- **Cider-Honey Twist:** Replace the white wine with apple cider and add a teaspoon of honey for a sweet and tart alternative.
- **Herb Infusion:** Infuse the cream with fresh thyme or tarragon for an aromatic lift.
- **Spice Adventure:** Add a pinch of cayenne pepper or smoked paprika to the sauce for a kick of heat and smokiness.

HEALTH NOTE & CALORIC INFORMATION
This hearty French dish, while rich in flavor, also comes with a significant calorie count. A single serving, including the bread, could weigh in at approximately 600-800 calories. The heavy cream and sausage are the primary sources of fat. However, by making dairy-free and low-fat modifications, one can lower the calorie content and fat intake.

NIÇOISE PISSALADIÈRE

Pissaladière originated from Nice in the Provence-Alpes-Côte d'Azur region of France. This dish is a testament to the simple yet profound flavors of Provençal cuisine, historically served as a snack or light lunch. With its caramelized onions, anchovies, and olives, it reflects the region's love for fresh, Mediterranean ingredients. A close relative to the Italian pizza, Pissaladière has been warming the hearts of locals and travelers alike since the 13th century, offering a savory slice of Niçoise tradition.

INGREDIENTS

- 500g all-purpose flour
- 10g active dry yeast
- 300ml warm water
- 2 tsp sugar
- 2 tsp salt
- 3 tbsp olive oil, plus extra for drizzling
- 1 kg yellow onions, thinly sliced
- 2 cloves garlic, minced
- 2 tbsp fresh thyme leaves, chopped
- 200g anchovy fillets
- 100g Niçoise or Kalamata olives, pitted
- Freshly ground black pepper

DIRECTIONS

1. In a large mixing bowl, combine the yeast, sugar, and warm water. Allow it to sit for 5-10 minutes until it becomes frothy, indicating that the yeast is active.
2. Add 2 tablespoons olive oil, flour, and salt to the yeast mixture. Mix until a dough begins to form.
3. Transfer the dough onto a floured surface and knead for about 10 minutes until smooth and elastic.
4. Place the dough in a clean, oiled bowl, cover with a damp cloth, and let it rise for about 1 hour or until doubled in size.
5. In the meantime, heat 1 tablespoon of olive oil in a large pan over medium heat. Add the onions and a pinch of salt, cooking them slowly for about 30 minutes until they are caramelized and golden. Halfway through cooking, add the minced garlic and thyme and continue to cook.
6. Preheat your oven to 220°C (425°F).
7. Once the dough has risen, punch it down and roll it out on a floured surface to fit a rectangular baking sheet. Transfer the dough to the sheet.
8. Spread the caramelized onion mixture evenly over the dough, leaving a small border around the edges.
9. Decoratively place the anchovy fillets over the onions, and scatter the olives on top. Drizzle a little olive oil over the top and add a few grinds of black pepper.
10. Bake for 15-20 minutes or until the crust is golden and crisp.
11. Serve warm, cut into squares or strips.

DIETARY MODIFICATIONS

Vegetarian: Substitute the anchovy fillets with sun-dried tomatoes to maintain a similar umami profile. Capers can also be added to enhance the savory quality of the dish.

Vegan: Follow the vegetarian substitutions, and use a vegan dough (ensure the sugar is also vegan). For the caramelized onions, use vegan butter instead of olive oil for a richer flavor.

Gluten-Free: Replace the all-purpose flour with a gluten-free blend designed for bread. Ensure that the yeast is gluten-free, and be prepared to adjust the amount of water as gluten-free doughs can require different hydration levels.

INGREDIENT SPOTLIGHT: ANCHOVY FILLETS

Anchovy fillets are an essential element in Pissaladière, introducing a punch of umami flavor that defines this dish. Anchovies have been used in European cuisine since the Roman times, where they were fermented into a sauce called garum. Today, anchovies are found in a variety of culinary applications, from Caesar salad dressing to Worcestershire sauce. Their salty, intense flavor profile complements the sweetness of the caramelized onions, making them irreplaceable in Pissaladière.

CHEF'S TIPS

- Patience is key with onions. Cook them slowly to encourage a deep caramelization without burning.
- Use a pizza stone if available for an even crispier crust.
- For a more traditional Pissaladière, roll the dough slightly thicker to achieve a typical bread-like base.
- If the dough is proving too elastic and difficult to roll, let it rest for 5 to 10 minutes to relax the gluten.
- Fresh thyme can be substituted with dried thyme, but reduce the quantity by half, as the flavor is more concentrated when dried.

POSSIBLE VARIATIONS OF THE RECIPE

- **Herbed Pissaladière:** Incorporate a mix of Provençal herbs into the dough and sprinkle on top before baking for an extra layer of aromatic flavor.
- **Cheesy Pissaladière:** Prior to baking, sprinkle a generous amount of grated Gruyère or another melting cheese over the onions for a gooey, rich topping.
- **Fig and Walnut Pissaladière:** For a sweet and savory take, top the caramelized onions with sliced fresh figs and toasted walnuts before baking. This variation omits the anchovies.

HEALTH NOTE & CALORIC INFORMATION

A slice of Pissaladière is rich in carbohydrates from the dough and provides a moderate amount of protein from the anchovies.

It is also a good source of healthy fats, particularly if you use high-quality olive oil.

A standard serving may contain approximately 250-350 calories, with variations depending on the size of the slice and any additional toppings.

CLASSIC CHERRY CLAFOUTIS

Clafoutis, pronounced klah-foo-TEE, hails from the Limousin region of France. With a history dating back to the 19th century, it's a beloved rustic dessert that typically features black cherries baked in a smooth, flan-like batter. Enjoyed warm, it's both simple and elegant, embodying the charm of French countryside cooking.

INGREDIENTS

- 500g fresh black cherries, pitted
- 4 large eggs
- 1 cup (240ml) whole milk
- 2/3 cup (130g) granulated sugar
- 1 teaspoon vanilla extract
- 1/2 cup (70g) all-purpose flour
- Pinch of salt
- Powdered sugar for dusting
- Butter, for greasing the pan

DIRECTIONS

1. Preheat your oven to 350°F (175°C). Butter a 9-inch round baking dish generously.
2. Spread the pitted cherries in a single layer across the bottom of the prepared dish.
3. In a medium bowl, whisk together the eggs and granulated sugar until light and frothy.
4. Add the vanilla extract and mix well.
5. Sift the flour and salt into the egg mixture. Whisk until just combined and smooth.
6. Whisking continuously, gradually add the milk to the batter until fully integrated and smooth.
7. Pour the batter over the cherries in the baking dish.
8. Place the baking dish in the oven and bake for 35-45 minutes, or until the clafoutis is set and golden brown on top.
9. Remove from the oven and let cool slightly.
10. Dust with powdered sugar before serving. Clafoutis is traditionally enjoyed warm.

DIETARY MODIFICATIONS

Gluten-Free: Replace all-purpose flour with almond flour or a gluten-free flour blend. Ensure that the blend is designed for 1:1 substitution to maintain the structure and texture of the clafoutis.

Lactose Intolerance: Substitute whole milk with lactose-free milk or a non-dairy milk alternative like almond, soy, or coconut milk. The consistency might change slightly, but the clafoutis should still set up nicely.

Vegan: Create a vegan batter by using a non-dairy milk, a vegan sugar that hasn't been processed with bone char, and replacing the eggs with a mixture of silken tofu (1/4 cup per egg), apple cider vinegar, and baking soda to maintain the custard-like texture.

INGREDIENT SPOTLIGHT: CHERRIES

The cherry, particularly the black variety, is the soul of this dessert. Native to the Caspian-Black Sea region, they've been cultivated since prehistoric times. Cherries are praised for their sweet-tart flavor that infuses the clafoutis with a delightful contrast against the creamy batter. Nutritionally rich in antioxidants like anthocyanins, they provide not just taste but health benefits, too. The juicy burst from the cooked cherries provides a unique texture and flavor that's irreplaceable in this dish.

CHEF'S TIPS

- For an authentic touch, leave the cherry pits in; they're said to impart a subtle almond flavor as they bake.
- Ensure all ingredients are at room temperature before mixing for a more homogenous batter.
- Do not overmix the batter after adding flour to avoid a tough texture.
- To prevent a soggy bottom, make sure the cherries are dry before you lay them in the dish.
- Serve clafoutis moderately warm to best enjoy its custardy texture and the juicy cherries.

POSSIBLE VARIATIONS OF THE RECIPE

- **Stone Fruit Clafoutis:** Swap cherries with other stone fruits like apricots, peaches or plums, chopped if large, to enjoy a different but equally delicious flavor profile.
- **Berry Clafoutis:** Use a mix of berries such as blueberries, raspberries, and blackberries for a more tart clafoutis and a beautifully colorful dessert.
- **Chocolate & Pear Clafoutis:** For a richer twist, add chocolate chips to the batter, and arrange slices of pear in place of cherries for a decadent combination.

HEALTH NOTE & CALORIC INFORMATION

A serving of cherry clafoutis contains approximately 200-250 calories, with a good balance of macronutrients. The cherries provide fiber and vitamins, while the milk and eggs supply protein and fat. It's a dessert with a relatively moderate glycemic index due to the fruit content and should be consumed as part of a balanced diet.

FLAMMEKUECHE, ALSO KNOWN AS TARTE FLAMBÉE

Originating from the historical region on the French-German border called Alsace, Flammekueche is a traditional dish that reflects a blend of both cultures. The name translates to "flame cake" in Alsatian dialect, hinting at its method of cooking in a wood-fired oven. It was originally a dish made by bakers to test the heat of their ovens, but its deliciousness quickly turned it into a regional favorite, now enjoyed in restaurants and homes alike.

INGREDIENTS

- 250g all-purpose flour
- 1 tsp salt
- 1 tsp instant yeast
- 150ml warm water
- 2 tbsp olive oil
- 200g crème fraîche or fromage blanc
- 1 small onion, thinly sliced
- 100g smoked bacon, cut into small strips
- Salt and pepper, to taste
- A pinch of nutmeg (optional)

DIRECTIONS

1. In a large bowl, combine the flour, salt, and instant yeast. Make a well in the center and add the warm water and olive oil. Mix until a dough forms.
2. Knead the dough on a floured surface for about 5-7 minutes until it becomes smooth and elastic.
3. Place the dough back in the bowl, cover with a towel, and let it rest in a warm place for about 1 hour or until it doubles in size.
4. Preheat your oven to the highest setting, around 250°C (480°F), and if you have a baking stone, place it in the oven now. If not, use an inverted baking tray.
5. On a floured surface, roll out the dough into a thin, rectangular shape, roughly 30x40 cm (12x16 inches).
6. Carefully transfer the rolled-out dough onto a piece of parchment paper.
7. Spread the crème fraîche or fromage blanc evenly over the dough, leaving a slight border around the edges.
8. Scatter the thinly sliced onions and bacon strips over the crème fraîche.
9. Season with salt, pepper, and a pinch of nutmeg if desired.
10. Slide the Flammekueche with the parchment paper onto the preheated baking stone or inverted tray.
11. Bake for 10-15 minutes until the edges are crispy and lightly browned.
12. Slice and serve hot, straight out of the oven.

DIETARY MODIFICATIONS

Vegetarian: Replace the smoked bacon with a vegetarian alternative like sliced mushrooms, which provide a meaty texture. You can also add a bit of smoked paprika to mimic the smokiness of bacon.

Vegan: For a vegan version, use a dairy-free sour cream substitute in place of the crème fraîche and a vegan bacon alternative or smoked tofu. Ensure the dough does not contain animal products.

Dairy-Free: Substitute the crème fraîche with lactose-free sour cream or a dairy-free alternative such as coconut-based yogurt to maintain the creamy texture without lactose.

INGREDIENT SPOTLIGHT: CRÈME FRAÎCHE

Crème fraîche is a thick cultured cream with a slightly tangy and nutty flavor, which is essential in Flammekueche. It originated in France and is similar to sour cream but less sour and with a higher fat content, allowing it to withstand high temperatures without curdling. It lends a velvety texture and a rich taste that balances the smoky bacon and sharp onions in the recipe. For this dish, it creates the iconic creamy base that distinguishes Flammekueche from other flatbread dishes.

CHEF'S TIPS

- For an authentic taste, try to find Alsatian smoked bacon, known for its distinct flavor.
- Do not overwork the dough; a light touch will ensure a crispier base.
- Roll the dough as thin as possible for the classic Flammekueche experience.
- Preheating the baking surface is critical for a crisp bottom crust.
- Serve immediately after baking to enjoy the contrast of the crispy crust with the creamy topping.

POSSIBLE VARIATIONS OF THE RECIPE

- **Sweet Flammekueche:** For a dessert version, replace the savory toppings with thinly sliced apples, sprinkle with cinnamon and sugar, and bake. Serve with a dollop of whipped cream or vanilla ice cream.
- **Seafood Flammekueche:** Replace the smoked bacon with smoked salmon or trout, capers, and a sprinkle of dill for a pescatarian twist on this classic.
- **Cheese Lover's Flammekueche:** Add grated Munster or Gruyère cheese over the crème fraîche before adding the onions and bacon for an extra cheesy delight.

HEALTH NOTE & CALORIC INFORMATION

A typical serving of Flammekueche contains approximately 500-600 calories, with the majority of calories coming from the dough and crème fraîche. It is also a source of protein from the bacon and has carbohydrates from the flour. This dish can be considered high in fat due to the crème fraîche and bacon, but by adjusting toppings and portion sizes, it can fit into a balanced diet.

GALETTE BRETONNE

Hailing from the region of Brittany in France, the Galette Bretonne, or Breton galette, is a savory crêpe made with buckwheat flour. This dish has been a staple of French cuisine since the Middle Ages, with the hearty use of buckwheat being a testament to its durability and popularity among the people of Brittany, where wheat was scarce. Versatile and nourishing, it forms a perfect canvas for a variety of fillings, traditionally ham, cheese, and egg.

INGREDIENTS

- 1 cup buckwheat flour
- 1 3/4 cups water
- 1 egg
- 1/4 teaspoon salt
- Butter for cooking
- 1/4 pound high-quality ham, thinly sliced
- 1 cup grated Gruyère cheese
- 4 eggs (one for each galette)
- Freshly ground black pepper
- Chopped fresh chives for garnish

DIRECTIONS

1. In a large bowl, whisk together the buckwheat flour, water, one egg, and salt until smooth, forming the galette batter. Let it rest for 2 hours at room temperature.
2. Heat a large non-stick skillet or crêpe pan over medium heat. Add a small knob of butter and coat the bottom of the pan.
3. Pour a ladleful of batter into the center of the pan. Quickly tilt and rotate the pan to spread the batter into a thin, even layer.
4. Cook for about 1 minute or until the edges start to lift from the pan. Using a spatula, flip the galette and cook for another 30 seconds.
5. Place slices of ham and a generous sprinkle of cheese on half of the galette, leaving a small border around the edge.
6. Crack an egg onto the center of the galette and spread it slightly with a fork, being careful not to break the yolk.
7. Fold the two sides of the galette over the filling, then the top and bottom to form a square shape, leaving the yolk exposed.
8. Continue to cook until the cheese is melted and the egg white is set but the yolk remains runny, about 2 minutes.
9. Slide the galette onto a plate, season with black pepper, and sprinkle with chives.
10. Repeat with the remaining batter and fillings to make four galettes.

DIETARY MODIFICATIONS

Vegetarian: Substitute the ham with sautéed mushrooms or spinach to maintain the savory character of the galette. The mushrooms, especially, will add a meaty texture.

Vegan: Replace the buckwheat batter egg with 1 tablespoon of flaxseed meal mixed with 3 tablespoons of water. Use vegan cheese and skip the egg topping, or experiment with a dollop of seasoned tofu scramble instead.

Gluten Sensitivity: Fortunately, buckwheat is naturally gluten-free—ensure that your buckwheat flour is labeled as such to avoid cross-contamination from processing facilities.

INGREDIENT SPOTLIGHT: BUCKWHEAT FLOUR

Buckwheat Flour: Despite its name, buckwheat is not related to wheat and is naturally gluten-free. It's a fruit seed related to rhubarb and sorrel. Buckwheat has been grown in Brittany since the 15th century and became the grain of choice due to the region's harsh climate, where traditional wheat could not thrive. Its nutty flavor gives galettes their distinctive taste and hearty texture. The flour is a good source of protein, fiber, and energy, and it is key to making authentic galettes.

CHEF'S TIPS

- Resting the batter allows the buckwheat flour to fully hydrate, yielding a more consistent crepe texture.
- Use medium heat to cook the galettes, as high heat can cause them to cook too quickly and become brittle rather than pliable.
- Use clarified butter to grease the pan if available; it has a higher smoke point and will make your galettes less prone to burning.
- For a perfectly runny yolk, ensure the egg is at room temperature before cracking it onto the galette.
- Serve immediately after cooking to enjoy the galette with the best texture and flavor.

POSSIBLE VARIATIONS OF THE RECIPE

- **Seafood Delight:** For a coastal twist, add smoked salmon, capers, and a dollop of crème fraîche instead of ham and cheese.
- **Sweet Switch:** Transform the galette into a dessert by using regular flour, adding sugar to the batter, and filling it with stewed apples and a sprinkle of cinnamon.
- **Deluxe Galette:** Pile on luxury by using flavors such as caramelized onions, goat cheese, sun-dried tomatoes, and a sprinkle of fresh herbs.

HEALTH NOTE & CALORIC INFORMATION

Eating galettes offers a good balance of protein, fiber, and nutrients, particularly when filled with a variety of vegetables or lean proteins. A single galette with ham, cheese, and egg may contain approximately 400-500 calories, with buckwheat providing valuable micronutrients such as manganese, copper, and magnesium. Remember, modifications to the fillings will alter the nutritional content accordingly.

BLANQUETTE DE VEAU
CLASSIC FRENCH VEAL STEW

Blanquette de Veau is a staple of French cuisine, cherished for its creamy sauce and tender pieces of veal. Its name is derived from "blanc," referring to the white sauce devoid of browning the meat—a technique common in French cooking. Beloved since the 18th century, it's often served during family gatherings and important events, symbolizing the warmth and richness of French culinary tradition.

INGREDIENTS

- 1 kg veal shoulder, cut into large chunks
- 1 large onion, studded with 3 cloves
- 2 carrots, sliced
- 2 leeks, white part only, cut into large pieces
- 1 celery stalk, cut into pieces
- 1 bouquet garni (thyme, bay leaf, parsley)
- Salt and black pepper to taste
- 2 liters water or veal stock
- 60 g butter
- 60 g all-purpose flour
- 200 ml heavy cream
- 1 large egg yolk
- Juice of half a lemon
- 200 g button mushrooms, quartered
- Fresh parsley, chopped for garnish

DIRECTIONS

1. Begin by preparing your veal and vegetables. Rinse the veal and pat it dry with paper towels.
2. In a large pot, bring the water or veal stock to a simmer. Add the veal chunks, onion with cloves, carrots, leeks, celery, and bouquet garni. Season with salt and pepper.
3. Let the pot simmer gently for 1.5 hours, skimming any foam or impurities that rise to the surface periodically.
4. Once the meat is tender, remove it along with the vegetables, straining the cooking broth through a fine sieve. Discard the onion and bouquet garni.
5. In the same pot, melt butter over medium heat. Add flour, stirring constantly for about 2 minutes to create a roux.
6. Gradually whisk in the strained cooking broth until the sauce thickens. Simmer for about 10 minutes, continuing to stir.
7. In a small bowl, mix the heavy cream and egg yolk. Temper this mixture by slowly adding a few tablespoons of the hot sauce, stirring constantly. After tempering, add the mixture back into the pot, stirring well.
8. Add the lemon juice and adjust seasoning as necessary.
9. Return the veal and vegetables (except the onion and bouquet garni) to the pot. Add the quartered mushrooms.
10. Let everything warm through for about 10 minutes on low heat.
11. Before serving, sprinkle with fresh parsley. Serve with rice or steamed potatoes.

DIETARY MODIFICATIONS

Vegetarian: Replace veal with firm tofu or tempeh cut into cubes. Use vegetable stock instead of veal stock and ensure that you press tofu to remove excess moisture before searing it lightly to maintain some texture when simmering in the stew. The rest of the recipe remains unchanged.

Vegan: Follow the vegetarian modifications, but also substitute the butter with plant-based butter, the heavy cream with coconut cream, and omit the egg yolk. Consider adding a tablespoon of nutritional yeast for a richer flavor.

Lactose Intolerance: Use lactose-free butter or margarine and lactose-free cream. The egg yolk does not contain lactose and can be included without modification.

INGREDIENT SPOTLIGHT: BOUQUET GARNI

The bouquet garni is a classical French bouquet of herbs, traditionally consisting of fresh parsley, thyme, and bay leaf, though recipes may vary. It's often tied together with string and used to infuse broths, stews, and soups with complex aromas and depths of flavor. The practice of using bouquet garni dates back to the 17th century, enhancing the subtlety and fragrance of French cuisine without leaving leafy textures in the dish. Particularly in Blanquette de Veau, the bouquet garni plays a crucial role, imparting its delicate herbs' essence into the stew without overpowering the main ingredients.

CHEF'S TIPS
- Do not rush the simmering process; slow cooking is key to tender meat and rich flavors.
- For a velvety sauce, be sure to skim the fat and impurities that rise to the top during simmering.
- A roux can easily burn, so keep the heat medium and stir continuously for an evenly cooked, lump-free sauce.
- When tempering the cream mixture, add the hot liquid slowly to prevent the eggs from curdling.
- If the sauce is too thick after adding all ingredients, thin it with a bit more stock or water.

POSSIBLE VARIATIONS OF THE RECIPE
- **Mushroom Medley:** Add a mix of gourmet mushrooms such as shiitake, chanterelle, or porcini instead of regular button mushrooms for an earthier, more robust flavor.
- **Wine-Infused:** Enhance the sauce by adding a splash of white wine during the simmering process, allowing the alcohol to cook off and the stew to take on a subtle fruity note.
- **Seafood Blanquette:** Substitute veal with firm fleshed fish like cod or scallops, and shrimp for a lighter take on the classic, reducing the simmering time accordingly to avoid overcooking the delicate seafood.

HEALTH NOTE & CALORIC INFORMATION
A serving of Blanquette de Veau typically contains approximately 600-700 calories, with a substantial amount of protein from the veal, and fats coming from the butter and cream. It's also a good source of vitamins and minerals present in the vegetables. However, given its richness, portion control should be considered for those tracking calorie intake or dietary fat.

SALADE LYONNAISE

Hailing from Lyon, France, a city often considered the gastronomic capital, Salade Lyonnaise is a classic French bistro dish. This salad artfully combines the rich textures and flavors of poached eggs and crispy bacon with the fresh bite of frisée lettuce, all dressed in a warm, tangy vinaigrette. It's a hearty yet elegant dish that showcases the Lyon's appreciation for refined yet simple cuisine.

INGREDIENTS

- Frisée lettuce, 1 large head (or substitute with curly endive)
- Thick-cut bacon, 200g (about 6 slices)
- Shallots, 2, finely chopped
- Red wine vinegar, 3 tablespoons
- Dijon mustard, 1 tablespoon
- Olive oil, 2 tablespoons
- Eggs, 4
- Salt, to taste
- Freshly ground black pepper, to taste
- Croutons (optional, for garnish)
- Chopped fresh herbs (like parsley or chervil, optional, for garnish)

DIRECTIONS

1. **Prepare the Lettuce:** Clean the frisée lettuce thoroughly, discarding the tough outer leaves. Tear the tender leaves into bite-sized pieces and spin dry. Set aside in a large mixing bowl.
2. **Cook the Bacon:** Cut the bacon into lardons (small strips or cubes). In a skillet over medium heat, cook the bacon pieces until golden and crisp, about 5 minutes. Using a slotted spoon, transfer them to a paper towel-lined plate to drain. Keep the bacon fat in the skillet.
3. **Make the Vinaigrette:** In the same skillet with bacon fat, lower the heat and add the shallots. Cook until they are soft, about 2 minutes. Pour in the red wine vinegar to deglaze the skillet, scraping up any browned bits from the bottom. Stir in the Dijon mustard and whisk while gradually adding the olive oil to create an emulsion. Season with salt and pepper to taste.
4. **Poach the Eggs:** Fill a saucepan with several inches of water and bring to a gentle simmer. Add a small splash of vinegar, which helps the egg whites coalesce. Break an egg into a small bowl or cup and slide it into the simmering water gently. Repeat with the remaining eggs. Poach until the whites are set but yolks remain runny, about 3 to 4 minutes. Remove the eggs with a slotted spoon to a paper towel-lined plate to drain excess water.
5. **Assemble the Salad:**
   - Toss the warm bacon and vinaigrette with the frisée lettuce until evenly coated. Taste and adjust seasoning if necessary.
   - Divide the dressed lettuce among plates. Carefully top each with a poached egg. Add croutons and chopped herbs for garnish if desired.
   - Serve immediately, with the expectation that diners will break the egg, allowing the yolk to further dress the salad.

DIETARY MODIFICATIONS

Vegetarian: Replace the bacon with smoked tempeh or a plant-based bacon substitute that has been sliced into pieces. Follow the same cooking instructions to achieve a similar smoky, crispy texture.

Vegan: Along with the vegetarian substitution for bacon, replace the poached eggs with a vegan egg product, or opt for sliced avocado to add creaminess. Use a vegan Dijon mustard if the original contains honey.

Gluten-free: Ensure that the bacon, Dijon mustard, and any additional garnishes such as croutons are certified gluten-free or made from gluten-free ingredients.

INGREDIENT SPOTLIGHT: DIJON MUSTARD

Dijon Mustard originated in the city of Dijon, the capital of Burgundy, France. It's known for its pale yellow color and creamy consistency. Made from brown mustard seeds and white wine or a mix of wine vinegar, water, and salt, Dijon mustard lends a tangy, sharp, and slightly spicy flavor to vinaigrettes and sauces. In this recipe, Dijon mustard is key as it emulsifies the dressing, providing a creamy texture and a depth of flavor that balances the richness of the bacon and the soft egg yolk.

CHEF'S TIPS

- Freshness Counts: Use the freshest eggs available for poaching as they hold their shape better in the water.
- Lettuce Selection: If frisée is unavailable, curly endive or even baby arugula can work as substitutes, providing the desired bitter crispness.
- Gentle Bacon Cooking: Cook the bacon on medium heat to render the fat without burning it, which is essential for a flavorful vinaigrette.
- Vinaigrette Warmth: Make sure the vinaigrette is warm when tossing it with the salad; this helps the flavors meld together and slightly wilts the lettuce.
- Poaching Perfection: Create a gentle whirlpool in the simmering water before adding the egg to help the white wrap around the yolk.

POSSIBLE VARIATIONS OF THE RECIPE

- Salade Niçoise Influence: Add elements such as anchovies, tomatoes, and black olives for a Provencal twist.
- Autumnal Version: Introduce roasted butternut squash, walnuts, and blue cheese crumbles for a heartier, seasonal salad.
- Mediterranean Inspiration: Include crispy chickpeas, sun-dried tomatoes, and a sprinkle of feta cheese for a Mediterranean take.

HEALTH NOTE & CALORIC INFORMATION

A traditional Salade Lyonnaise contains approximately 400-600 calories per serving, depending on the bacon portion and dressing amount. It is rich in protein from the egg and bacon, and provides a variety of nutrients including vitamins A and K from the frisée lettuce. However, it can also be high in fat, mostly from the bacon and olive oil. Adjusting portion sizes and ingredients can tailor the nutritional content to meet individual dietary goals.

CLASSIC FRENCH POT-AU-FEU

Pot-au-Feu, translating to "pot on the fire," is a French culinary staple with roots dating back to the Middle Ages. This humble peasant dish has been embraced by all social classes for its comforting qualities and simplicity. Traditionally, Pot-au-Feu is a family meal that brings everyone together on a Sunday to enjoy a slow-cooked, nourishing feast. It's not only a dish but an experience, often served in two parts: first the broth with vegetables, and then the meats with mustard and pickles.

INGREDIENTS

- 1 kg of beef chuck, cut into large chunks
- 500g of marrow bones
- 3 carrots, peeled and cut into chunks
- 3 leeks, white parts only, cleaned and cut into chunks
- 3 turnips, peeled and quartered
- 1 onion, studded with 2 cloves
- 4 garlic cloves, peeled
- 2 bay leaves
- A few sprigs of fresh thyme
- A few sprigs of parsley
- 1 whole nutmeg, for grating
- Salt and black pepper to taste
- Water to cover the ingredients in the pot

DIRECTIONS

1. Begin by rinsing the beef and bones under cold water to remove any bone fragments. Pat the meat dry with paper towels.
2. In a large stockpot, place the beef and marrow bones. Fill with enough cold water to cover the ingredients by at least an inch, then bring to a gentle boil over medium-high heat.
3. Once boiling, skim off any impurities that rise to the surface for a clear broth. Reduce the heat to low, ensuring a very gentle simmer.
4. Add the studded onion, garlic cloves, carrots, leeks, turnips, bay leaves, thyme, and parsley to the pot. Grate a little nutmeg over everything and season with salt and pepper.
5. Cover the pot with a lid slightly ajar and simmer for 3 to 4 hours, checking occasionally to skim off any impurities and adjust the seasoning if necessary.
6. When the meat is tender and the vegetables are soft, remove the pot from heat. Gently remove the beef, bones, and vegetables with a slotted spoon and transfer them to a serving platter.
7. Strain the broth through a fine sieve and serve it hot in bowls. The meat and vegetables can be served separately on the platter, ready to be enjoyed with coarse sea salt, Dijon mustard, and cornichons.

DIETARY MODIFICATIONS

Vegetarian: Replace beef and marrow bones with a mix of hearty root vegetables such as parsnips, extra turnips, and celeriac. Use vegetable broth instead of water and add umami flavor with soy sauce or miso paste.

Vegan: Follow the vegetarian modifications and make sure to use vegan-friendly condiments when serving, such as vegan mustard and pickles without any animal-derived ingredients.

Gluten-Free: This recipe is naturally gluten-free. However, always check the labels on mustard and other condiments for hidden gluten sources.

INGREDIENT SPOTLIGHT: MARROW BONES

Marrow bones play a starring role in our Pot-au-Feu. Marrow has been a prized ingredient since prehistoric times due to its high energy content and essential fatty acids. In this dish, it enriches the broth with a luxurious depth of flavor and offers buttery morsels to spread on toast. Marrow bones also contribute to the body and gelatinous quality that makes Pot-au-Feu's broth so distinctive and satisfying after a slow simmer.

CHEF'S TIPS

- Make this dish a day ahead—the flavors meld and deepen when the broth and ingredients have time to rest and cool together.
- Always start with cold water for a clear and impurity-free broth. It allows the proteins to coagulate slowly and rise to the top, making skimming easier.
- Be patient with the simmering process. A gentle, barely-there bubble is key to tender meat and a clear broth.
- For a richer broth, roast the bones in the oven until golden before adding them to the pot.
- Serve the Pot-au-Feu with toasted baguette slices to soak up the delicious broth and marrow.

POSSIBLE VARIATIONS OF THE RECIPE

- **Cozy Winter Pot-au-Feu:** Add a quartered cabbage and some smoked sausage during the last hour of cooking for a smokier, heartier version.
- **Spring Vegetable Pot-au-Feu:** Lighten up the dish by using chicken instead of beef and include spring vegetables like peas, asparagus, and baby carrots.
- **Exotic Pot-au-Feu:** Infuse the broth with spices like star anise, cinnamon, and ginger. Serve with fresh herbs such as cilantro and a side of hoisin sauce for an Asian twist on the French classic.

HEALTH NOTE & CALORIC INFORMATION

A typical serving of Pot-au-Feu is rich in protein and collagen due to the beef and marrow bones. The broth is low in carbohydrates and, depending on the amount of vegetables used, can be a good source of fiber. The dish is relatively high in fat, especially if marrow is consumed. A standard serving without marrow could average around 500-600 calories. Including marrow would increase the calorie count due to its high-fat content. Always remember that these numbers can vary widely depending on the portion size and specific ingredients used.

PROVENCAL BRANDADE DE MORUE

Brandade de Morue is a classic dish from the Provence region of France, famed for its rich and cultural food heritage. It is a luxurious blend of salt cod (morue), olive oil, garlic, and milk or cream. Historically, this dish was a means for preserving codfish before the advent of refrigeration. With trade routes bringing salt from the Mediterranean and cod from the Atlantic, Brandade de Morue became a perfect marriage of these commodities. Its comforting texture and layered flavors make it a beloved dish among locals and a treasured recipe in French cuisine.

INGREDIENTS

- 500g salted cod, soaked and desalted
- 3-4 garlic cloves, finely minced
- 250ml whole milk
- 250ml heavy cream
- 2 bay leaves
- 100ml extra virgin olive oil
- Juice of 1/2 lemon
- 1 small bunch of parsley, chopped
- Black pepper, to taste
- Crusty bread or roasted potatoes, for serving

DIRECTIONS

1. The evening before, place the salted cod in a large bowl with cold water, changing the water several times over 24 hours to desalt the fish completely.
2. Once desalted, drain and pat the cod dry with a clean cloth or paper towels.
3. In a large saucepan, combine the milk, cream, and bay leaves. Bring to a gentle simmer over low heat.
4. Add the salt cod to the milk mixture and poach gently for 15 minutes, or until the fish is tender and flakes easily.
5. Carefully remove the cod from the milk mixture, setting the milk aside, and discard the bay leaves.
6. In another bowl, flake the cod with a fork, removing any bones or skin.
7. In a mortar and pestle or with a mixer, combine the flaked cod, garlic, and a little of the reserved milk, and begin to crush or beat together.
8. Slowly incorporate the olive oil in a steady stream as if making mayonnaise, until the mixture is smooth and emulsified.
9. Add lemon juice, parsley, and black pepper; adjust seasoning, adding more milk if needed for a creamier texture.
10. Serve the brandade warm with crusty bread for spreading or alongside roasted potatoes.

DIETARY MODIFICATIONS

Gluten-Free: Serve with gluten-free bread or over naturally gluten-free sides like roasted potatoes, rice, or gluten-free toast points.

Lactose-Free: Substitute the whole milk and cream with lactose-free alternatives like lactose-free milk and cream or almond or soy milk for a less traditional but still creamy texture.

Pescatarian-Friendly: This dish is already pescatarian. Ensure that all other ingredients, such as the bread served with the brandade, also meet pescatarian standards.

INGREDIENT SPOTLIGHT: SALTED COD

The spotlight ingredient in this dish is the salted cod. With a history that traces back hundreds of years, salted cod was a crucial commodity during the age of exploration, providing a stable source of protein on long sea voyages. Its preservation technique allowed it to be transported and stored without spoiling, finding its way into various cuisines across Europe, the Caribbean, and South America. In Brandade de Morue, salted cod is not only the protein centerpiece but also the source of the dish's unique, savory depth, which is balanced by the creamy, garlic-infused base.

CHEF'S TIPS

- Begin desalting the cod well in advance, ideally 24-36 hours ahead, to ensure the fish is not overly salty.
- When emulsifying the fish with olive oil, add the oil very slowly to avoid separation and achieve a smooth, creamy texture.
- Poach the fish gently to preserve its delicate texture; aggressive boiling can make it tough.
- Use a good quality extra virgin olive oil for the best flavor, as it is a defining component of the dish.
- If you don't have a mortar and pestle or a mixer, a sturdy fork or whisk and some elbow grease will suffice to blend the mixture to the right consistency.

POSSIBLE VARIATIONS OF THE RECIPE

- **Brandade with Potatoes:** For a heartier version, mix in some mashed potatoes to the brandade before baking it in the oven until golden on top.
- **Spicy Brandade:** Add a pinch of cayenne or a few dashes of your favorite hot sauce to the mixture for a spicy kick.
- **Brandade Croquettes:** Use the brandade as filling for croquettes, breading, and frying them until crisp for a wonderful appetizer or snack.

HEALTH NOTE & CALORIC INFORMATION

Brandade de Morue is rich in protein and omega-3 fatty acids due to the salt cod. However, it is also high in calories and fats because of the olive oil and cream. To reduce its calorie content, you may opt for lower-fat milk and cream options. For a typical serving, you can expect around 300-400 calories, depending on the portion size and the exact ingredients used.

CLASSIC FRENCH PORK RILLETTES

Rillettes, a dish with roots in the central Touraine and Sarthe regions of France, dates back to the 15th century. Initially a modest preparation meant to preserve pork before the advent of refrigeration, it has evolved into a gourmet spread celebrated for its rich, savory flavor and tender texture. Typically found in the form of pork, though other meats like duck can also be used, it's perfect for a charcuterie board or spread on crusty bread.

INGREDIENTS

- 2 lbs boneless pork shoulder, cut into 2-inch pieces
- 8 oz pork belly, cut into 2-inch pieces
- 2 teaspoons salt
- 1 teaspoon freshly ground black pepper
- 1 teaspoon ground allspice
- 2 bay leaves
- 4 sprigs of fresh thyme
- 3 cloves of garlic, minced
- 2 cups rendered pork lard or duck fat
- Crusty bread, for serving
- Cornichons and whole-grain mustard, for serving

DIRECTIONS

1. In a large bowl, combine the pork shoulder, pork belly, salt, pepper, and allspice. Mix well to ensure the meat is evenly coated. Cover and refrigerate for at least 2 hours or overnight to marinate.
2. Transfer the marinated pork to a large Dutch oven or heavy-bottomed pot. Add the bay leaves, thyme, and minced garlic to the pot.
3. Gently melt the rendered pork lard or duck fat in a separate pan and then pour over the pork until it's completely submerged.
4. Cover the pot and cook on the lowest possible heat for about 3 to 4 hours. You want to maintain a very gentle simmer, where the meat slowly confits in the fat until it's extremely tender and can be easily shredded.
5. Once the meat is tender, remove the bay leaves and thyme sprigs. Use two forks to shred the pork mixture into a paste within the pot, removing any gristly pieces.
6. Transfer the shredded meat into sterilized jars, pressing down to pack it in without air pockets. Pour enough of the cooking fat over the meat to cover it by about half an inch.
7. Seal the jars and refrigerate until the fat solidifies and forms a cap. The rillettes can be stored in the refrigerator for several weeks.
8. To serve, allow the rillettes to come to room temperature. Spread on slices of crusty bread and enjoy with cornichons and whole-grain mustard.

DIETARY MODIFICATIONS

Vegetarian: Replace the pork with a mix of hearty vegetables such as portobello mushrooms, eggplants, and artichokes. Sauté these in olive oil with similar herbs and spices, then chop or shred the cooked vegetables before preserving in a sterilized jar with a layer of olive oil on top.

Low Fat: For a lower fat version, consider using chicken breast meat instead of pork and substituting chicken stock for the majority of the lard or fat. Be aware that this will significantly change the texture and flavor profile of the dish.

Gluten-Free: The rillettes themselves are naturally gluten-free, however, ensure that they are served with gluten-free bread or crackers to accommodate this dietary need.

INGREDIENT SPOTLIGHT: RENDERED PORK LARD

Rendered pork lard is the traditional cooking fat used to make rillettes. It not only serves to confit the pork, cooking it to tender perfection, but also to preserve it. The pork shoulder is slowly cooked in its own fat, which later solidifies and seals the meat in jars, preventing air (and bacteria) from spoiling the product. Culinary historians suggest that lard has been used this way for centuries, particularly in peasant farming communities where no part of an animal was wasted.

CHEF'S TIPS

- To develop more flavor, consider toasting the spices slightly before marinating the meat.
- Keep your heat low! Patience yields the perfect texture. If the meat cooks too fast, it will become tough rather than tender and spreadable.
- When shredding the meat, make sure to remove any tough sinew or cartilage that didn't break down during cooking.
- To ensure longevity, leave ample fat to cover the meat when jarring—this seals out bacteria and preserves the rillettes.
- Let your rillettes age in the fridge for a few days before eating; this will allow the flavors to meld together even more.

POSSIBLE VARIATIONS OF THE RECIPE

- **Duck Rillettes:** Use duck legs in place of pork for a richer, gamey flavor. The process is similar, just adjust the cooking time as needed for the duck to become tender.
- **Herbed Goat Cheese Rillettes:** For a non-meat version, mix goat cheese with finely diced sun-dried tomatoes, olives, garlic, and a variety of herbs. Refrigerate and serve as a flavorful vegetarian spread.
- **Spicy Rillettes:** Add a kick to your rillettes by including a mix of your favorite chili peppers or pepper flakes during the cooking process for a spicier variant.

HEALTH NOTE & CALORIC INFORMATION

Rillettes are a high-fat, high-calorie food. A single serving of two tablespoons can contain around 200 calories, mostly from fat. The dish is low in carbs and provides a moderate amount of protein. It's rich in B-vitamins and minerals such as selenium, depending on the meat used. As a dense source of calories, it should be enjoyed in moderation as part of a balanced diet.

QUENELLES DE BROCHET À LA LYONNAISE

Quenelles de Brochet is a French dish with deep roots in the cuisine of Lyon, often considered the gastronomic capital of France. Quenelle refers to the mixture of creamed fish, usually pike (brochet in French), with breadcrumb and egg, typically poached and served with a rich sauce such as Nantua sauce, made with crayfish. The elegant and smooth texture of the dish makes it a refined emblem of French culinary sophistication. It praises the tradition of using local, freshwater fish and displaying the delicate art of French cooking techniques.

INGREDIENTS

- 400g pike fillet (skinless and boneless)
- 240ml whole milk
- 2 slices of white bread (crusts removed)
- 2 large eggs
- 1 large egg yolk
- A pinch of freshly grated nutmeg
- Salt and white pepper to taste
- 2 tablespoons butter (plus extra for greasing)
- For the Nantua Sauce:
- 300ml fish stock
- 200ml heavy cream
- 100g crayfish tails
- 50g unsalted butter
- 1 tablespoon brandy
- 1 tablespoon tomato paste
- Salt and cayenne pepper to taste
- Fresh parsley for garnish

DIRECTIONS

1. Start by preheating your oven to 180°C (355°F).
2. In a saucepan, heat the milk until warm, not boiling. Soak the bread slices in milk until fully saturated, then squeeze out excess milk.
3. Combine the pike fillet with the moistened bread, eggs, egg yolk, nutmeg, salt, and white pepper in a food processor. Blend until you have a smooth mixture.
4. Transfer the mixture to a bowl and beat with a wooden spoon for about 5 minutes to aerate it; this will give the quenelles a lighter texture.
5. Bring a large pot of salted water to a gentle simmer.
6. Using two spoons dippped in cold water, shape portions of the fish mixture into ovals (quenelles) and gently drop them into the simmering water.
7. Poach the quenelles for about 10-12 minutes, or until they rise to the surface and are firm to the touch.
8. Remove the quenelles with a slotted spoon and drain on a kitchen towel. Arrange them in a buttered ovenproof dish.
9. Prepare the Nantua Sauce by combining the fish stock, heavy cream, crayfish tails, butter, brandy, and tomato paste in a saucepan.
10. Cook over medium heat until the sauce coats the back of a spoon, season with salt and cayenne pepper.
11. Pour the Nantua Sauce over the quenelles in the dish and dot with extra butter.
12. Bake in the preheated oven for 10-15 minutes until bubbling and lightly golden on top.
13. Garnish with fresh parsley before serving.

DIETARY MODIFICATIONS

Vegetarian: Replace pike with a firm tofu that's been drained and pressed for a vegetarian version of the dish. Use unsweetened almond milk and a flaxseed mixture (1 tablespoon ground flaxseeds with 3 tablespoons water per egg) as a binding agent.

Lactose Intolerance: Opt for lactose-free milk and cream. Also, ensure that the butter used is lactose-free or substitute with lactose-free margarine.

Gluten-Free: Use gluten-free bread for the mixture, and ensure that your fish stock and other sauce ingredients are gluten-free.

INGREDIENT SPOTLIGHT: PIKE FISH

Pike is a freshwater fish valued for its lean, firm texture, preferred for making quenelles because of its ability to bind well with other ingredients without overpowering the dish. Pike has a long history in European cuisine, capable of yielding large, meaty fillets, making it an ideal candidate for the delicate and refined nature of quenelles. A key reason why pike is used in this recipe is its ability to create a smooth, homogenous mixture which is essential for achieving the classic, mousse-like consistency of quenelles.

CHEF'S TIPS

- Ensure that the fish is very fresh, as older fish may adversely affect the delicate flavor of the quenelles.
- Beat the mixture vigorously; this incorporates air and makes the quenelles lighter.
- Shape the quenelles as uniformly as possible to ensure even cooking.
- The quenelles should be poached at a gentle simmer to prevent them from breaking apart.
- If the Nantua sauce becomes too thick after adding to the oven, thin it out with a little fish stock or water to reach the desired consistency.

POSSIBLE VARIATIONS OF THE RECIPE

- **Modern Twist:** Incorporate smoked salmon into the quenelle mixture for a smoky, modern flavor variant.
- **Cheese Lovers:** Add finely grated Gruyère cheese to the mixture before poaching for a rich, cheesy depth.
- **Herb Infusion:** Mix finely chopped fresh tarragon or dill into the quenelle mixture for an aromatic twist.

HEALTH NOTE & CALORIC INFORMATION

Quenelles de Brochet à la Lyonnaise is rich in protein, provided by the pike and eggs. However, it is also high in fat due to the cream and butter in both the quenelles and the Nantua sauce. A single serving can have upwards of 400 calories, the majority of which will come from fats. For a lighter version, one could reduce the cream and butter quantities and substitute some of the ingredients with low-fat or fat-free options. This classic French dish is also a good source of various vitamins and minerals from the fish and crayfish, including B-vitamins and phosphorus.

PROVENCAL FOUGASSE
WITH OLIVES AND HERBS

Fougasse is a traditional bread originating from the Provence region in France. Its distinctive ladder shape was historically used to test the temperature of wood-fired ovens; if the fougasse baked correctly, the oven was ready for the main batch of bread. Over time, it has evolved from a simple flatbread to incorporate various flavors like olives, herbs, and cheeses, reflecting the rustic and aromatic cuisine of the South of France.

INGREDIENTS

- 500g strong white bread flour
- 7g fast-action dried yeast
- 2 tsp salt
- 1 tsp sugar
- 300ml lukewarm water
- 2 tbsp extra virgin olive oil
- 100g pitted Kalamata olives, chopped
- 2 tbsp fresh rosemary, chopped
- 2 tbsp fresh thyme, chopped
- Coarse sea salt, for sprinkling
- Olive oil, for drizzling

DIRECTIONS

1. In a large bowl, mix together the flour, yeast, salt, and sugar.
2. Make a well in the center and pour in the lukewarm water and olive oil.
3. Gradually mix the flour into the liquids to form a rough dough.
4. Turn out the dough onto a lightly floured surface and knead for about 10 minutes until smooth and elastic.
5. Place the dough in a lightly oiled bowl, cover with a damp cloth, and let it rise in a warm place for 1 hour, or until doubled in size.
6. Turn the risen dough onto a floured surface and knead in the olives and herbs until evenly distributed.
7. Line a baking sheet with parchment paper. Shape the dough into a flat, oval shape and place onto the prepared sheet.
8. Using a sharp knife, make a series of diagonal cuts through the dough, creating the traditional ladder pattern. Gently pull apart the cuts to open the holes slightly.
9. Cover with a cloth and let it rise for another 30 minutes.
10. Preheat your oven to 220°C (425°F).
11. Once risen, drizzle the fougasse with olive oil and sprinkle with coarse sea salt.
12. Bake in the preheated oven for 15-20 minutes or until golden brown and hollow sounding when tapped.
13. Cool on a wire rack before serving.

DIETARY MODIFICATIONS

Vegan: Replace the sugar with agave syrup or another vegan sweetener, and ensure the olives are not prepared with any non-vegan additives.

Gluten-Free: Use a gluten-free flour blend designed for bread baking. You may need to adjust the amount of water as gluten-free blends tend to absorb moisture differently.

Low-Sodium: Reduce the salt in the dough to 1 teaspoon and omit the additional coarse sea salt sprinkled on top before baking.

INGREDIENT SPOTLIGHT: KALAMATA OLIVES

Kalamata olives are the jewel of Greek olives, cherished for their fruity, rich flavor and meaty texture. They are typically deep purple and harvested in the Kalamata region of the Peloponnese peninsula. These olives are a key ingredient in Mediterranean diets, offering healthy fats and antioxidants. In fougasse, they provide bursts of savory flavor that complement the aromatic herbs, enhancing the Provençal character of the bread.

CHEF'S TIPS

- When kneading the dough, use a push-and-fold method to develop gluten, which gives the bread its chewy texture.
- Ensure your water is lukewarm—too hot and it will kill the yeast, too cold and the yeast won't activate properly.
- Be gentle when incorporating the olives and herbs to avoid deflating the dough.
- For extra flavor, you can soak the olives in a mixture of olive oil and herbs overnight before adding them to the dough.
- If the bread is browning too quickly in the oven, loosely cover it with foil to prevent burning.

POSSIBLE VARIATIONS OF THE RECIPE

- **Cheese Lover's Fougasse:** Before the final rise, knead in 100g of grated Gruyère or Comté cheese into the dough.
- **Mediterranean Version:** Include sundried tomatoes and a pinch of dried oregano along with the olives and fresh herbs.
- **Sweet Fougasse:** For a dessert variation, skip the olives and herbs, add zest of 1 orange and a handful of dried cranberries, and dust with powdered sugar after baking.

HEALTH NOTE & CALORIC INFORMATION

A typical serving of fougasse (about 1/8 of the loaf) contains roughly 250-300 calories. This bread is a source of carbohydrates and provides small amounts of protein and fiber. The olives contribute healthy monounsaturated fats. However, those watching their salt intake should enjoy fougasse in moderation due to the salty olives and the sea salt topping.

BAECKEOFFE
(ALSATIAN MEAT AND POTATO STEW)

Baeckeoffe is a traditional Alsatian dish, which translates to "baker's oven." It is a mix of marinated meats and vegetables, slow-cooked to perfection, reminiscent of a French version of a casserole. The story goes that Alsatian housewives would prepare the dish on Saturday evenings, take it to the local baker on Sunday morning while they attended church, and then pick it up afterwards for a hearty lunch. The long, slow cooking would result in tender meat and a flavorful stew, perfect for the family gathering.

INGREDIENTS

- 500g beef chuck, cut into large cubes
- 500g pork shoulder, cut into large cubes
- 500g lamb shoulder, cut into large cubes
- 750g potatoes, peeled and sliced
- 3 onions, thinly sliced
- 2 leeks, white part only, thinly sliced
- 3 garlic cloves, minced
- 2 carrots, sliced
- 750ml dry white Alsatian wine (e.g., Riesling)
- 2 bay leaves
- 1 tsp thyme
- 1 tsp juniper berries
- Salt and pepper to taste
- 2 tbsp parsley, chopped
- 1 tbsp sunflower oil

DIRECTIONS

1. **Marinate:** In a large bowl, combine the beef, pork, and lamb with the white wine, garlic, bay leaves, thyme, juniper berries, salt, and pepper. Cover and refrigerate for at least 12 hours.
2. **Prep Veggies:** Preheat your oven to 160°C (325°F). Oil a large casserole dish and begin layering with half of the sliced potatoes, onions, leeks, and carrots.
3. **Assemble:** Retrieve the marinated meat, and place it on top of the vegetable layer with its marinade. Add the remaining potatoes, onions, leeks, and carrots. Season with a little more salt and pepper.
4. **Cook:** Cover the casserole dish with its lid or aluminum foil. Bake in the preheated oven for 3 to 4 hours, or until the meat is very tender and the veggies are cooked through.
5. **Serve:** Sprinkle with chopped parsley before serving. Enjoy your Baeckeoffe with a side of green salad and a glass of leftover Alsatian wine.

DIETARY MODIFICATIONS

Vegetarian: Substitute meats with a mix of mushrooms, jackfruit, and chickpeas for a similar hearty texture. Use vegetable broth instead of wine for marination.

Vegan: Follow the vegetarian substitutes and ensure to abstain from any meat, dairy, or animal-derived ingredients. Use olive oil for greasing the casserole.

Gluten-free: The recipe is naturally gluten-free. However, ensure that the wine used for marination is gluten-free, as some wines may contain gluten-based fining agents.

INGREDIENT SPOTLIGHT: JUNIPER BERRIES

Juniper berries are the small, dark berries of the juniper bush, noticeable in this recipe for adding a distinct aromatic and slightly piney flavor. Originating from regions in Europe, they're long esteemed for their medicinal and culinary uses, particularly in game dishes and gin production. In the context of Baeckeoffe, juniper berries fuse with the wine's flavors and meat's richness, introducing a note that's hard to replicate, making them indispensable for authenticity.

CHEF'S TIPS

- **Quality Wine:** Use a high-quality, aromatic Alsatian wine like Riesling or Gewürztraminer for marination; the dish's flavor depends significantly on it.
- **Searing:** For added flavor, sear the meat in a hot pan before marinating to develop a deeper flavor.
- **Tight Seal:** Traditionally, the lid of the casserole would be sealed with dough to trap moisture. For home cooks, ensure the foil or lid provides a tight seal.
- **Resting Time:** Let the Baeckeoffe rest for 10 minutes before serving to allow the flavors to settle.
- **Marination Time:** For the meat to fully absorb the flavors, marinate for at least 12 hours, though 24 hours would be ideal.

POSSIBLE VARIATIONS OF THE RECIPE

- **Seafood Baeckeoffe:** Replace meats with a mix of fish and shellfish for a pescatarian twist on the traditional stew.
- **Spicy Baeckeoffe:** Add sliced chili peppers or a spoonful of Dijon mustard into the marinade for those who like a bit of heat in their dish.
- **Winter Vegetable Baeckeoffe:** Utilize seasonal root vegetables like turnips, parsnips, and sweet potatoes for a vegetarian winter alternative to the classic.

HEALTH NOTE & CALORIC INFORMATION

Baeckeoffe is hearty and rich, providing a substantial amount of protein from the various meats used. Depending on the cuts of meat and the amount of oil used, a single serving can be relatively high in fat. The vegetables add fiber, vitamins, and minerals. A serving can range around 600-800 calories, taking into account the rich nature of the stew and the inclusion of wine. Always consider portion size and balance the meal with lighter side dishes.

FAR BRETON

Far Breton is a traditional custardy cake from Brittany, a region in the northwest of France. It's a rich and indulgent dish that is as much at home at a casual afternoon tea as it is concluding an elegant dinner. The roots of Far Breton date back to the 18th century, where it started as a savory dish before evolving into the sweet and plump prune-filled dessert we know today.

INGREDIENTS

- 1 cup (140g) pitted prunes
- 3 tablespoons (45ml) rum
- 2 cups (480ml) whole milk
- 4 large eggs
- 1/2 cup (100g) granulated sugar
- 1 teaspoon (5ml) vanilla extract
- 1 pinch of salt
- 1 cup (120g) all-purpose flour
- Powdered sugar for dusting (optional)
- Butter for greasing the pan

DIRECTIONS

1. Preheat your oven to 350°F (175°C). Grease a 9x9 inch (23cm square) baking dish with butter.
2. In a small bowl, soak the prunes in rum for at least 1 hour to allow them to plump up and absorb the flavor.
3. Warm the milk in a saucepan over medium heat just until it begins to steam. Do not boil. Remove from heat and let cool slightly.
4. In a large mixing bowl, whisk the eggs and granulated sugar together until the mixture becomes light and frothy.
5. Add the vanilla extract and a pinch of salt to the egg mixture, continuing to whisk until fully combined.
6. Sift the flour into the egg mixture, whisking continuously to avoid lumps.
7. Gradually incorporate the warm milk into the batter, whisking until you have a smooth, thin batter.
8. Drain the prunes from the rum, and scatter them evenly across the bottom of the greased baking dish.
9. Pour the batter carefully over the prunes in the baking dish.
10. Bake for 40-50 minutes, or until the Far Breton is golden and a skewer inserted into the center comes out clean.
11. Allow the Far Breton to cool in the pan. Once cooled, dust with powdered sugar if desired, and serve.

DIETARY MODIFICATIONS

Gluten-free: Substitute the all-purpose flour with a gluten-free flour blend. Ensure that the blend is a 1:1 replacement to maintain the texture of the cake.

Lactose intolerance: Use lactose-free milk as a direct substitute for the whole milk to make this dessert lactose-friendly while keeping its creamy consistency.

Vegan: Replace the eggs with 4 tablespoons of ground flaxseed mixed with 12 tablespoons of water and let sit until thickened. Use a plant-based milk alternative for the whole milk and swap the butter for vegan butter or oil.

INGREDIENT SPOTLIGHT: PRUNES

Prunes are the spotlight ingredient in this recipe. Dried plums, as they're also known, have a history of being consumed since ancient times, originally found in areas near the Caspian Sea. They're known for their sweetness and health benefits, including aiding digestion. In Far Breton, prunes add not only a chewy texture but also a depth of flavor that complements the dense, custard-like batter.

CHEF'S TIPS

- If the prunes are very dry, you may need to soak them for several hours or overnight to ensure they're plump and juicy.
- Warm the milk to just below boiling; this helps it blend smoothly into the batter without cooking the eggs.
- To avoid deflating the whipped eggs and sugar, sift the flour in gently and fold it through rather than whisking vigorously.
- Check the Far Breton a few minutes before the timer goes off; it should be just set to keep the custardy texture.
- Serve the Far Breton at room temperature to best enjoy its flavors and textures.

POSSIBLE VARIATIONS OF THE RECIPE

- **Far Breton with Tea-Soaked Prunes:** Steep the prunes in hot black tea instead of rum for a subtler flavor that still gives a nod to Brittany's Celtic connections.
- **Chocolate Far Breton:** Add 1/4 cup of cocoa powder to the flour for a chocolate version. Chocolate complements prunes exceptionally well.
- **Apple Far Breton:** Substitute the prunes with thinly sliced apples and a teaspoon of cinnamon to give it an autumnal twist.

HEALTH NOTE & CALORIC INFORMATION

A typical serving of Far Breton contains approximately:
- 210 calories,
- 6 grams of fat,
- 34 grams of carbohydrates,
- 6 grams of protein.

It also provides essential nutrients such as calcium and iron, courtesy of the milk and eggs.

SOCCA NIÇOISE

Originating from the sun-kissed coastline of Nice in France, Socca is a beloved street food that has captivated palates for centuries. This simple yet delightful chickpea flatbread mirrors the Mediterranean's affinity for humble ingredients morphing into rustic elegance. Socca's history is as rich as its nutty flavor, with Italian roots that can be traced back to Genoa where it is known as 'farinata.' This dish unites cultures and continues to be a staple in the Ligurian Sea region, cherished for its crisp edges, soft center, and versatile nature.

INGREDIENTS

- 1 cup chickpea flour (also known as gram flour or besan)
- 1 cup water
- 2 tablespoons olive oil, plus more for the pan
- 1/2 teaspoon salt
- Freshly ground black pepper, to taste
- Optional: Rosemary or thyme for garnish

DIRECTIONS

1. In a mixing bowl, whisk together the chickpea flour and salt.
2. Gradually pour in the water while continuing to whisk, ensuring a lump-free batter.
3. Stir in 2 tablespoons of olive oil and a generous amount of freshly ground black pepper. Let the batter rest for at least 30 minutes, allowing the flour to absorb the water and the flavors to meld.
4. Preheat your oven's broiler to high and position a rack about 6 inches from the heat source.
5. In a cast-iron skillet or ovenproof non-stick pan, pour enough olive oil to coat the bottom lightly and heat it over medium-high heat until shimmering.
6. Pour the batter into the pan to form a thin layer, similar to a crepe.
7. Cook the flatbread for about 3-5 minutes until the bottom is golden and edges start to crisp up.
8. Transfer the skillet to the oven and broil for 3-4 minutes until the top is browned and blistered.
9. Remove the socca from the oven, let it cool slightly, then slide or flip it onto a cutting board.
10. Cut into wedges, garnish with rosemary or thyme if desired, and serve warm.

DIETARY MODIFICATIONS

Gluten-Free: Chickpea flour is inherently gluten-free, making socca an excellent choice for those with gluten intolerance or celiac disease.

Vegetarian/Vegan: Socca is completely plant-based, so it's already suitable for vegetarians and vegans without any modifications.

Low-FODMAP: To adapt Socca for a low-FODMAP diet, ensure that the chickpea flour is allowed within their guidelines or use a FODMAP-friendly legume flour alternative and omit any high-FODMAP garnishes.

INGREDIENT SPOTLIGHT: CHICKPEA FLOUR

Chickpea flour is the crown jewel of this recipe. Also known as gram flour or besan, it is made from ground chickpeas and boasts a high protein content, fiber, and a suite of essential nutrients. Its origins are rooted in Indian, Middle Eastern, and Mediterranean cuisines. The use in socca highlights its versatility, acting as a gluten-free flour option that imparts a subtly sweet and nutty flavor, essential to achieving the classic character of socca. Chickpea flour is also popular in vegan cooking as an egg substitute when mixed with water.

CHEF'S TIPS

- Rest the batter: Allowing the batter to rest is crucial as it hydrates the flour, yielding a more tender flatbread.
- Use a high-quality olive oil: As one of the few ingredients, its flavor will shine through, so opt for the best you can get.
- Achieve the right consistency: The batter should be similar to heavy cream; adjust with water or flour as necessary.
- Preheat your pan: A hot pan helps in forming a crispy, golden crust on the bottom.
- Watch closely under the broiler: Broiling can go from perfectly golden to burnt in seconds. Keep an eye on the socca during the final minutes of cooking.

POSSIBLE VARIATIONS OF THE RECIPE

- **Herbed Socca:** Mix in finely chopped fresh herbs like rosemary, thyme, or parsley into the batter before cooking for an aromatic twist.
- **Spicy Socca:** For those who enjoy a bit of a kick, add a pinch of cayenne pepper or red chili flakes to the batter before cooking.
- **Cheesy Socca:** After broiling, sprinkle freshly grated Parmesan or Pecorino cheese over the hot socca and return to the oven for a melty, cheesy top layer.

HEALTH NOTE & CALORIC INFORMATION

A single traditional socca flatbread is a good source of protein and fiber while being naturally gluten-free. It contains healthy fats from olive oil, and the main ingredient, chickpea flour, contributes vitamins and minerals like folate, iron, and magnesium. A typical serving size (1/4 of the recipe) contains approximately 180 calories, 10 grams of healthy fats, 5 grams of protein, and 18 grams of carbohydrates.

MOUCLADE

Mouclade is a quintessentially French dish with a twist—the traditional maritime flavor of mussels is elevated by the exotic warmth of curry. This dish reveals its origins from the coastal regions of France, where the fresh catch from the sea meets the spices brought by historical trade routes. Perfect for a light yet satisfying meal, Mouclade is a testament to the fusion of local produce with global flavors.

INGREDIENTS

- 2 kg (4.4 lbs) fresh mussels, cleaned and debearded
- 2 tablespoons unsalted butter
- 1 large onion, finely chopped
- 3 cloves of garlic, minced
- 1 bay leaf
- 2 teaspoons curry powder
- 300 ml (1¼ cups) dry white wine
- 150 ml (⅔ cup) heavy cream
- Salt to taste
- Freshly ground black pepper to taste
- A handful of fresh parsley, chopped
- Freshly squeezed juice of half a lemon
- Baguette, to serve

DIRECTIONS

1. In a large pot, melt the butter over medium heat.
2. Add the chopped onion and minced garlic, cooking until they are soft and translucent but not browned, for about 3 minutes.
3. Stir in the curry powder and bay leaf, and cook for another minute to release the flavors.
4. Pour in the dry white wine and bring to a simmer. Let it reduce slightly for about 2 minutes.
5. Add the cleaned mussels to the pot. Cover with a lid and steam until the mussels open, around 5 to 7 minutes. Be sure to shake the pot occasionally to ensure even cooking.
6. Once the mussels have opened (discard any that do not), use a slotted spoon to transfer them to a serving dish, leaving the liquid in the pot.
7. Add the heavy cream to the liquid in the pot and bring to a light simmer. Season with salt and black pepper. Simmer for 2-3 minutes to allow the sauce to thicken slightly.
8. Stir in the fresh parsley and lemon juice, then taste and adjust the seasoning if necessary.
9. Pour the curry sauce over the mussels in the serving dish.
10. Serve immediately with fresh baguette slices to soak up the delicious sauce.

DIETARY MODIFICATIONS

Lactose Intolerant: Replace the butter with olive oil or a lactose-free margarine, and use a lactose-free cream or full-fat coconut milk for the heavy cream.

Vegetarian: Substitute mussels with a combination of hearty vegetables such as mushrooms, eggplants, and zucchini. Follow the same cooking process, adjusting the cooking time accordingly for the vegetables to become tender.

Vegan: Along with the vegetarian modifications, use a plant-based butter alternative and a vegan cream or coconut cream instead of heavy cream for the sauce.

INGREDIENT SPOTLIGHT: CURRY POWDER

Curry powder is a blend of spices that often includes turmeric, cumin, coriander, ginger, and chili pepper. Originating from the Indian subcontinent, curry powder was adopted by the British during colonial rule and has since become a staple in numerous culinary traditions. In the case of Mouclade, curry powder adds a warm, slightly spicy and intricate flavor profile that brilliantly contrasts the fresh, briny quality of the mussels. This ingredient is key to bridging the flavors of land and sea.

CHEF'S TIPS
- Always buy fresh mussels from a reputable source and cook them the day you buy them to ensure the best quality and flavor.
- Before cooking, make sure to clean the mussels thoroughly by scrubbing the shells and removing the 'beards.' Discard any mussels that are already open and do not close when tapped.
- Do not overcook the mussels; they are done as soon as the shells open. Overcooking can result in chewy and tough mussels.
- For a more intense flavor, you can toast the curry powder in a dry pan before adding it to the dish.
- To add depth to the sauce, consider using a homemade fish stock in addition to or as a replacement for the white wine.

POSSIBLE VARIATIONS OF THE RECIPE
- Spicy Mouclade: Add a few pinches of red pepper flakes or a finely chopped chili pepper along with the curry powder for an extra kick.
- Citrusy Twist: For a different acidic note, swap the lemon juice for lime or even grapefruit juice and include some of the zest in the sauce.
- Cream-Free Mouclade: If you prefer a lighter version, omit the cream altogether and thicken the sauce with a bit of flour or cornstarch slurry at the end of cooking.

HEALTH NOTE & CALORIC INFORMATION
Mussels are a low-calorie protein source rich in vitamins and minerals, particularly vitamin B12 and selenium. The addition of heavy cream increases the calorie and fat content, but you can opt for a light cream or dairy-free alternative to reduce this. A single serving without bread typically contains around 400 calories, with a majority coming from the mussels and the cream-based sauce.

FRAISIER
(TRADITIONAL FRENCH STRAWBERRY CAKE)

A Fraisier is a classic French cake whose name is derived from "fraise," meaning strawberry. Its layered elegance, combining the freshness of strawberries with rich pastry cream, is a celebration of spring and is often enjoyed during the strawberry season. This dessert became a staple in French pâtisseries in the 20th century and is adored for its stunning presentation that showcases the ripe berries at their prime.

INGREDIENTS

- For the Sponge Cake (Génoise):
- 4 large eggs, room temperature
- 120g granulated sugar
- 120g all-purpose flour
- 40g unsalted butter, melted and cooled
- 1 teaspoon vanilla extract
- For the Mousseline Cream:
- 500ml whole milk
- 1 vanilla bean, split lengthwise and seeds scraped
- 4 large egg yolks
- 100g granulated sugar
- 40g cornstarch
- 200g unsalted butter, at room temperature (divided)
- For Assembly:
- 500g fresh strawberries, hulled and halved lengthwise
- Apricot jam or neutral glaze (for the finish)

DIRECTIONS

1. Preheat oven to 180°C/350°F. Grease, line a 23cm/9in round cake tin with parchment paper.
2. Begin by making the génoise sponge cake. In a large bowl, whisk together the eggs, granulated sugar, and vanilla extract. Place the bowl over a pot of simmering water (double boiler) and continuously whisk until the mixture is warm to the touch.
3. Remove the bowl from heat and, using an electric mixer, beat on high until the mixture is pale and has tripled in volume. This is known as the ribbon stage.
4. Sift in the flour and gently fold it into the egg mixture, careful not to deflate the batter.
5. Take a small amount of the batter and mix it with the melted butter, then fold this back into the main batter until fully incorporated.
6. Pour the batter into the prepared tin and smooth the top with a spatula. Bake for around 20-25 minutes, or until the cake is golden and springs back when gently pressed. Remove from the oven and let it cool on a wire rack.
7. To make mousseline cream, heat the milk with the vanilla bean and seeds in a saucepan over medium heat. Whisk the egg yolks in a seprate bowl, sugar, and cornstarch together.
8. Once the milk is hot (not boiling), remove the vanilla bean and pour half of the milk over the egg yolk mixture, whisking continuously. Then return the entire mixture to the saucepan and cook over medium heat, whisking constantly until the cream thickens.
9. Remove the cream from heat as soon as it starts to bubble. Allow it to cool to about 60°C (140°F), then whisk in half of the butter until smooth. Cover the cream with plastic wrap, pressing it directly onto the surface, and chill until completely cool.
10. Once the pastry cream is cool, beat in the remaining butter until the cream is light and fluffy. This is now your mousseline cream.
11. To assemble the Fraisier, slice the cooled sponge cake horizontally into two even layers. Place one layer into a springform or adjustable cake ring lined with acetate or parchment.
12. Arrange the halved strawberries, cut side facing out, against the sides of the mold. Pipe or spoon the mousseline cream to fill in the gaps between the strawberries and to cover the bottom layer of sponge.
13. Add a second layer of strawberries on top of the cream and then place the second sponge layer on top.
14. Spread a thin layer of mousseline on the top sponge and smooth out. Cover and refrigerate for at least 4 hours or until the cream is set.
15. To finish, gently heat some apricot jam and brush it over the top for a glossy appearance. Carefully release the cake from the mold, and serve.

DIETARY MODIFICATIONS

Gluten-Free: Substitute the all-purpose flour with your preferred gluten-free flour blend. Ensure that it includes a binding agent such as xanthan gum to mimic the structure provided by gluten.

Lactose-Intolerance: Use lactose-free butter and milk for both the Génoise and the mousseline cream. Most supermarkets offer suitable alternatives that can be used as direct replacements.

Vegan: This is a more challenging modification due to the heavy reliance on eggs and butter. Use a vegan sponge cake base, substitute the eggs in the mousseline cream with silken tofu or a vegan egg replacer, and use dairy-free butter and plant-based milk.

INGREDIENT SPOTLIGHT: STRAWBERRY

The humble strawberry is the star here, with its name etched into the title of this dessert. Strawberries have been savored since Roman times and come into season in spring and early summer. In a Fraisier, strawberries aren't merely an accent; they provide structure, aesthetic, and a burst of fresh, sweet flavor that balances the richness of the cream.

CHEF'S TIPS

- Make sure your eggs are at room temperature before whisking them to achieve maximum volume.
- When folding in flour to the Génoise batter, be gentle and swift to preserve airiness.
- For clean cuts of cake, heat up the knife blade with hot water, then dry it before each slice.
- Chill your cake mold before assembly to help the mousseline cream set quicker and hold the strawberry arrangement in place.
- When applying the apricot glaze, ensure it's warm and thin enough to brush without pressing down on the cake surface.

POSSIBLE VARIATIONS OF THE RECIPE

- **Flavor Variations:** Infuse the pastry cream with citrus zest or rose water instead of vanilla for a unique twist.
- **Chocolate Fraisier:** Spread a thin layer of chocolate ganache on top of the first sponge layer before adding the cream and strawberries for a decadent touch.
- **Fruit Variations:** Though not traditional, raspberries or peaches can replace strawberries for a different, yet equally delicious, flavor profile.

HEALTH NOTE & CALORIC INFORMATION

This Fraisier is a rich dessert, and a single serving provides approximately 320-400 calories, varying with slice size and precise ingredient choices. The main contributors to this calorie count are the butter and sugar in the cake and mousseline cream. It also contains significant amounts of cholesterol and saturated fats from the butter and eggs, and some vitamin C and fiber from the fresh strawberries.

CERVELLE DE CANUT
(SILK WORKER'S BRAIN)

Cervelle de Canut is a classic Lyonnaise specialty, hailing from the silk-weaving history of Lyon, France. The name intriguingly translates to "silk worker's brain," reflecting the dish's humble origins. It was a traditional spread enjoyed by the hard-working canuts (silk workers) during the 19th century. The blend of herbs and fresh cheese provided a protein-rich and affordable meal that sustained them through long working hours. Today, it is a beloved staple in Lyon's bouchons (small bistros) and is enjoyed as a flavorful spread or dip, showcasing the city's rich culinary heritage.

INGREDIENTS

- 250g fromage blanc
- 2 tablespoons crème fraîche
- 1 small shallot, finely chopped
- 2 cloves of garlic, minced
- 2 tablespoons chives, finely chopped
- 1 tablespoon parsley, finely chopped
- 1 teaspoon tarragon, finely chopped
- 1 tablespoon white wine vinegar
- 2 tablespoons extra-virgin olive oil
- Salt and freshly ground black pepper, to taste
- A pinch of chopped chervil or dill (optional)

DIRECTIONS

1. In a medium-sized bowl, combine the fromage blanc and crème fraîche until you achieve a smooth, creamy consistency.
2. Add the finely chopped shallot and minced garlic to the mixture.
3. Mix in the fresh herbs (chives, parsley, tarragon, and optionally chervil or dill).
4. Stir in the white wine vinegar and extra-virgin olive oil. Blend well to ensure all ingredients are evenly distributed.
5. Season the mixture with salt and freshly ground black pepper to taste. Adjust the seasoning as necessary, remembering that the flavors will meld together over time.
6. Cover and refrigerate for at least 1 hour, allowing the flavors to infuse the cheese.
7. Before serving, give the spread one final stir and adjust seasonings if required.
8. Serve chilled with crusty bread or toast points for dipping, and enjoy a taste of Lyon's history.

DIETARY MODIFICATIONS

Vegetarian: No modifications needed as the recipe is already vegetarian-friendly.

Vegan: Substitute fromage blanc with a vegan cream cheese alternative. Use plant-based sour cream instead of crème fraîche. Ensure all other ingredients are vegan-approved.

Lactose Intolerance: Opt for lactose-free fromage blanc and a lactose-free cream or dairy substitute for the crème fraîche. Many stores now stock lactose-free versions of dairy products.

INGREDIENT SPOTLIGHT: FROMAGE BLANC

Fromage blanc is a fresh cheese of French origin. Its name directly translates to "white cheese" due to its color. This cheese is smooth and creamy with a taste that is mild and slightly tangy, making it a versatile ingredient in both savory and sweet dishes. Fromage blanc has less fat content compared to cream cheese, making it a healthier alternative. It is a crucial element to the authentic Cervelle de Canut, providing the characteristic texture and flavor that ties the herbs and seasoning together in this traditional Lyonnais dish.

CHEF'S TIPS
- Ensure fromage blanc and crème fraîche are well-chilled before use to maintain the spread's firmness.
- Use fresh herbs for the best flavor; dried herbs can be used but will not provide the same zest.
- For an extra tangy flavor, you can add a squeeze of fresh lemon juice.
- Let the Cervelle de Canut rest in the fridge longer if time allows; this will deepen the infusion of flavors.
- Always taste and adjust the seasoning just before serving as the flavors will evolve when chilled.

POSSIBLE VARIATIONS OF THE RECIPE
- **Fiery Kick:** Add a teaspoon of finely chopped fresh jalapeño or a sprinkle of chili flakes to the mixture for a bit of heat.
- **Herbaceous Twist:** Introduce basil and mint alongside the traditional herbs for a summer-fresh variation.
- **Autumn Delight:** Add a touch of honey and roasted, crushed walnuts for a sweet and crunchy dimension perfect for fall.

HEALTH NOTE & CALORIC INFORMATION
A serving of Cervelle de Canut is relatively low in calories due to the use of fromage blanc which is less fatty than other cheeses. A typical serving contains approximately 100-150 calories, with moderate amounts of fat (mostly from the olive oil and crème fraîche), and is rich in protein. It is also a good source of calcium and beneficial probiotics due to the live cultures in the fromage blanc. Keep in mind that any modifications or additions to the recipe, such as substituting vegan cheese or adding nuts, will alter the nutritional content.

PROVENÇAL GROS SOUPER
(SEVEN COURSES OF CHRISTMAS EVE)

The Gros Souper is a heartwarming Provençal tradition that dates back centuries. Held on Christmas Eve, this feast comprises seven meatless dishes, representing the seven sorrows of the Virgin Mary, followed by 13 desserts symbolizing Christ and his apostles. The meal is steeped in symbolism and serves as both a humble abstention before the lavish Christmas Day feasts and as a time for family to gather. Our recipe nods to this sacred tradition with simplified courses that maintain the essence of this regional celebration.

INGREDIENTS

- 1.5 kg of mixed winter vegetables (e.g., squash, turnip, parsnips, carrots)
- 500 g of salt cod
- 250 g of swiss chard
- 400 g of fresh spinach
- 2 leeks
- 1 head of garlic
- 400 g white beans (pre-soaked or canned)
- 200 g spaghetti
- 200 g breadcrumbs
- 100 g black olives
- Olive oil
- Salt and pepper to taste
- Herbes de Provence
- 1 liter of vegetable broth
- Star anise, cloves, and fennel seeds (for broth)
- 4 fresh bay leaves
- 250 g plain flour
- 15 g fresh yeast
- Pinch of sugar
- Warm water (for dough)
- Dried fruits and nuts (for the 13 desserts)

DIRECTIONS

1. **The Vegetable Dish:** Chop the winter vegetables into bite-sized pieces and place in a roasting tray. Sprinkle with olive oil, herbes de Provence, salt, and pepper; roast at 200°C for about 40 minutes, or until tender.
2. **Salt Cod:** Desalt the salt cod by soaking it in cold water for 24 hours, changing the water several times. Once desalted, poach the cod gently in water with a bay leaf, clove, and star anise until just cooked through. Flake the fish carefully.
3. **Swiss Chard & Spinach:** Rinse the swiss chard and spinach and chop finely. Sauté with minced garlic, olive oil, and a pinch of salt until wilted. Set aside.
4. **White Beans:** If not using canned beans, cook the pre-soaked white beans in a pot of simmering water with a bay leaf, clove, and a whole peeled onion until tender. Season with salt towards the end.
5. **Pasta with Herbs:** Boil the spaghetti until al dente, then toss with sautéed leeks, garlic, and a sprinkle of herbes de Provence. Drizzle with olive oil before serving.
6. **Garlic Soup:** Gently simmer minced garlic in olive oil without browning. Add vegetable broth, fennel seeds, a bay leaf, salt, and pepper, and simmer for 20 minutes. Serve with a sprinkle of breadcrumbs on top.
7. **Pistou (Provençal Pesto):** In a pestle and mortar, crush a handful of basil leaves with garlic, salt, and black olives until you have a paste. Gradually mix in olive oil until the sauce has a creamy consistency. Serve alongside the vegetables and fish.

DIETARY MODIFICATIONS

Gluten-Free: Substitute the wheat pasta with a gluten-free version and use gluten-free breadcrumbs for the garlic soup. Ensure all additional ingredients, like herbes de Provence, are gluten-free.

Vegan: Replace the salt cod with a salted tofu or tempeh, marinated in seaweed flakes to mimic a 'fishy' flavor. Ensure to press extra water out of the tofu before marinating and use vegetable broth for all soup bases.

Lactose Intolerance: There are no dairy ingredients in the traditional Gros Souper dishes, making it naturally suitable for those with lactose intolerance.

INGREDIENT SPOTLIGHT: HERBES DE PROVENCE

Herbes de Provence is a mixture of dried herbs typical of the Provence region. The blend usually includes savory, marjoram, rosemary, thyme, oregano, and sometimes lavender. Each herb contributes its unique flavor, creating a taste of the French countryside. Herbes de Provence was found in most French kitchens by the 1970s, but it's believed that the mixture was created in the 1950s or '60s to cater to the tastes of tourists visiting the region. This herb blend is key for our Gros Souper's vegetable dish, as it infuses the roast vegetables with the signature essence of Provençal cuisine.

CHEF'S TIPS

- Ensure you start desalting the salt cod well in advance — it is crucial to the final taste and texture of the fish.
- When roasting the vegetables, add the denser root vegetables first, as they will take longer to cook.
- For pasta with herbs, always reserve some pasta water to adjust the sauce's consistency if needed.
- Invest in a good quality olive oil for use in the Pistou and dressing; it greatly enhances the dish's flavors.
- Overcooking can destroy the subtle flavors of the Provençal herbs; always add them towards the end of the cooking process.

POSSIBLE VARIATIONS OF THE RECIPE

- **Mediterranean Twist:** Incorporate some roasted red peppers and artichokes to the vegetable dish, and finish it with a sprinkle of feta cheese (omit for vegan version).
- **Pescatarian Delight:** Add shrimps or other seafood to the Garlic Soup, creating a Bouillabaisse-esque dish fitting for the festive Christmas Eve.
- **Spicy Version:** Introduce a little heat to the dishes with the addition of red pepper flakes in the vegetables and a spicy version of Pistou with added chili.

HEALTH NOTE & CALORIC INFORMATION

The Gros Souper, while sumptuous, is rooted in modesty and, as such, is relatively light in calories compared to other festive meals. The meal is rich in vegetables and utilizes olive oil instead of butter — adhering to Mediterranean dietary practices known for their health benefits. The calories for such a meal can range significantly based on portion sizes but expect an average of 600-800 calories per serving for the entire seven-course affair. Rich in fibers, vitamins, and healthy fats, it's a heart-healthy banquet that respects tradition and taste.

TARTE DE BLETTES
(SWISS CHARD PIE)

Tarte de Blettes is a classic dish from the southeastern region of France, particularly from Nice in Provence. It is a testament to the versatility of Swiss chard, showcasing it in a way that balances sweet and savory, a common theme in Provençal cuisine. Traditionally served during Christmas, this dish is nonetheless enjoyed year-round. It's a prime example of how French cooks don't let any part of the plant go to waste, featuring the leafy greens as well as the more robust stems.

INGREDIENTS

- 2 bunches of Swiss chard, stems and leaves separated
- 1 roll of puff pastry or shortcrust pastry
- 100g golden raisins
- 3 tablespoons pine nuts
- 3 large eggs
- 200g ricotta cheese
- 100g grated Parmesan cheese
- 1 large onion, finely chopped
- 2 cloves of garlic, minced
- Zest of 1 lemon
- 2 tablespoons olive oil
- Salt and pepper, to taste
- Powdered sugar for dusting (optional)

DIRECTIONS

1. Preheat your oven to 180°C (355°F).
2. Blanch the Swiss chard leaves in boiling water for 1 minute and then transfer them to an ice water bath to stop the cooking process. Squeeze out the excess water and chop the leaves coarsely.
3. In a large pan, sauté the onion and Swiss chard stems with olive oil over medium heat until the onions are translucent and the stems begin to soften, about 10 minutes.
4. Add the garlic to the pan and sauté for another 2 minutes.
5. In a large bowl, mix the sautéed onion and Swiss chard stems with the chopped leaves, ricotta, Parmesan, eggs, lemon zest, pine nuts, and raisins. Season with salt and pepper.
6. Roll out the pastry and fit it into a 9-inch pie dish. Trim the excess pastry from the edges.
7. Pour the Swiss chard mixture into the pastry shell and spread it evenly.
8. Bake in the preheated oven for 35-40 minutes or until the filling is set and the crust is golden brown.
9. Allow to cool slightly before serving. Dust lightly with powdered sugar if desired.

DIETARY MODIFICATIONS

Vegetarian: The recipe is already vegetarian-friendly.

Vegan: Replace the eggs with a flaxseed or chia seed mixture (1 tablespoon of ground seeds mixed with 3 tablespoons of water equals one egg). Use vegan cheeses or tofu as a substitute for ricotta and Parmesan.

Lactose Intolerance: Opt for lactose-free cheese alternatives that mimic the texture and flavor of ricotta and Parmesan, or use lactose-free cottage cheese which has a similar consistency to ricotta.

INGREDIENT SPOTLIGHT: SWISS CHARD

Swiss chard is the star of this dish, an edible leafy green that is part of the beet family, consumed for its hearty leaves rather than its roots. With a history that traces back to Sicily, Swiss chard became a common ingredient in Mediterranean recipes. It brings not only a touch of color with its vibrant green leaves and red or yellow stems but also a wealth of nutrients, including vitamins A, C, and K. This recipe utilizes both the leaves and stems, giving the pie a rich texture and a beautiful rainbow of color.

CHEF'S TIPS
- Make sure to squeeze out as much water as possible from the blanched Swiss chard to prevent a soggy pie.
- Letting the Tarte de Blettes rest for a few minutes after baking will help it set, making it easier to slice.
- You can roast the pine nuts before adding them to the filling for an extra depth of flavor.
- If using store-bought pastry, opt for a butter-based version for richer flavor and flakier texture.
- Experiment with different cheese varieties to find your perfect blend—some might prefer a stronger cheese like Pecorino Romano.

POSSIBLE VARIATIONS OF THE RECIPE
- **Gluten-Free:** Use a gluten-free pastry crust or make your own with a blend of gluten-free flours.
- **Sweet Version:** For a sweeter variant, increase the raisins, add a bit of sugar to the filling, and infuse the pastry dough with a hint of vanilla extract.
- **Cheese Twist:** Incorporate a mix of different cheeses such as Gruyère or Emmental for a different flavor profile.

HEALTH NOTE & CALORIC INFORMATION
A typical serving of Tarte de Blettes offers a good balance of leafy greens and protein from the cheese and eggs. Swiss chard is low in calories but high in fiber, vitamins, and minerals. A slice of this pie provides energy from complex carbohydrates found in the pastry and has moderate amounts of fats, mostly coming from the cheese and olive oil. A single serving contains approximately 400-500 calories, with the variation depending on the specific quantities and types of cheese used, as well as the pastry type.

KOUIGN-AMANN
(BRETON BUTTER CAKE)

Originating from Brittany, France, in the 1800s, Kouign-Amann is a round, crusty cake made with a yeast dough and layers of butter and sugar folded in, similar to croissant dough. The name comes from the Breton language words for cake ("kouign") and butter ("amann"). This indulgent pastry has grown in popularity across France and globally for its delightful combination of sweet, buttery layers and a caramelized exterior.

INGREDIENTS

- 2 cups all-purpose flour, plus extra for dusting
- 1 cup unsalted butter, cold, plus 2 tbsp for greasing
- 1 tsp active dry yeast
- 2/3 cup warm water (around 110°F/43°C)
- 1 tsp salt
- 1 cup granulated sugar, plus extra for sprinkling

DIRECTIONS

1. Dough Preparation: In a small bowl, dissolve the yeast in warm water and let it sit until frothy, about 5-10 minutes.
2. In a large bowl, combine the flour and salt. Add the yeast mixture and stir until just combined into a dough.
3. Transfer the dough onto a lightly floured surface and knead for about 3-5 minutes until smooth. Form into a ball.
4. Place the dough in a lightly buttered bowl, cover with a clean cloth, and let it rise in a warm place for 1 hour or until doubled in size.
5. After the dough has risen, place it on a floured surface and roll it out into a large rectangle.
6. Layering Butter: Distribute small pats of cold butter over two-thirds of the rectangle, leaving a small margin around the edges. Sprinkle a third of the sugar over the butter.
7. Fold the unbuttered third of the dough over the middle third, then fold the opposite outer third over that (like folding a letter).
8. Turn the dough 90 degrees, roll it out again into a rectangle, sprinkle another third of the sugar, and fold it letter-style once more.
9. Wrap the dough in plastic wrap and refrigerate for 30 minutes.
10. Repeat the rolling, sugaring, and folding two more times, chilling the dough after each fold.
11. Preheat the oven to 375°F (190°C) and grease a muffin tin with butter.
12. Roll the dough out into a square about 1/4 inch thick. Cut the dough into 12 equal squares.
13. Place a square of dough in each muffin cup, sprinkle with a little more sugar, and let them rest for 20 minutes.
14. Baking: Bake for 30-40 minutes or until the pastries are golden brown and caramelized.
15. Let the Kouign-Amann cool for a few minutes before removing them from the muffin tin.

DIETARY MODIFICATIONS

Vegetarian: This recipe is inherently vegetarian so no modifications are needed.

Vegan: Substitute the butter with vegan butter or a solid coconut oil. Replace the warm water with a plant-based milk alternative warmed to the appropriate temperature.

Lactose Intolerance: Use lactose-free butter or margarine as a direct substitute for traditional butter in this recipe.

INGREDIENT SPOTLIGHT: BUTTER

Butter is the star of Kouign-Amann, not just for its role in the layers, but also in providing the rich, caramelized exterior which is integral to the pastry's character. The quality of the butter can greatly impact the flavor; traditionally, a high-fat, European-style butter is recommended for its lower water content and richer taste. Originating from pastoral cultures that valued dairy, butter has a long history, with evidence of its use dating back to 2000 BCE in butter sculptures of ancient India.

CHEF'S TIPS

- Use a rolling pin and firm pressure to evenly distribute the butter within the dough during the layering steps.
- Keep the dough as cold as possible to maintain the distinct layers of dough and butter. If it becomes too warm, return it to the refrigerator to firm up.
- Ideally, use a digital scale to ensure accurate measurements of ingredients, especially for the flour and sugar.
- For a more intense flavor, you can use salted butter, but be sure to omit the added salt from the recipe.
- To achieve the signature caramelization, do not be afraid to let the pastries bake until they are a deep golden brown.

POSSIBLE VARIATIONS OF THE RECIPE

- **Chocolate Kouign-Amann:** Add a small piece of high-quality dark chocolate in the center of each dough square before baking.
- **Fruit-Infused Kouign-Amann:** Add thinly sliced apples or pears atop the sugared layer during the second folding for a fruity twist.
- **Spiced Kouign-Amann:** Incorporate a mixture of cinnamon and nutmeg into the sugar before sprinkling it onto the dough for a spiced version.

HEALTH NOTE & CALORIC INFORMATION

One Kouign-Amann typically contains around 300-400 calories, with a majority coming from carbohydrates and fats, particularly saturated fats due to the high butter content. While delicious, they should be enjoyed in moderation within a balanced diet due to their high sugar content and lack of significant protein or fiber.

CLASSIC FRENCH PÂTÉ EN CROÛTE

Pâté en Croûte, or "meatloaf in a crust," is a quintessentially French dish that elegantly combines rich, savory filling with a flaky pastry crust. Dating back to medieval times when preserving meats was a necessity, this dish allowed for both preservation and presentation. A mainstay in charcuterie, Pâté en Croûte represents the art of French cooking and is often featured in festive settings and as a gourmet appetizer.

INGREDIENTS

For the Pastry:
- 2 1/2 cups all-purpose flour, plus extra for dusting
- 1/2 tsp salt
- 2 sticks (226 grams) unsalted butter, cold and cubed
- 6-8 tbsp ice water

For the Filling:
- 1 lb (450 grams) pork shoulder, finely diced
- 1/2 lb (225 grams) chicken liver, trimmed and finely chopped
- 1/4 lb (110 grams) smoked bacon, finely diced
- 2 cloves garlic, minced
- 2 shallots, finely chopped
- 3 tbsp brandy
- 2 tbsp fresh parsley, chopped
- 2 tsp fresh thyme, leaves only
- 1 tsp salt
- 1/2 tsp black pepper
- 1/4 tsp grated nutmeg
- 2 eggs, beaten

For Assembly and Glazing:
- 1 egg, for egg wash
- Gelatin (optional, for aspic)
- 1 cup chicken stock (if making aspic)

DIRECTIONS

1. Begin by making the pastry. In a large bowl, mix together flour and salt. Add the cold butter cubes and use your fingertips or a pastry blender to work it into the flour until you have a crumbly mixture. Gradually add ice water while stirring until the dough starts to come together.
2. Form the dough into a ball, wrap it in plastic wrap, and chill in the refrigerator for at least one hour.
3. While the dough is chilling, prepare the filling by combining the pork shoulder, chicken liver, bacon, garlic, shallots, brandy, parsley, thyme, salt, pepper, nutmeg, and one beaten egg in a large bowl. Mix thoroughly until well combined.
4. Preheat your oven to 375°F (190°C).
5. Roll out the dough on a floured surface to about 1/8 inch (3mm) thickness. Line a terrine mold or loaf pan with the pastry, allowing extra dough to hang over the edges.
6. Pack the filling into the pastry-lined mold, pressing down to remove air pockets.
7. Roll out the remaining dough to create the lid. Place the lid over the filling and crimp the edges to seal. Cut off any excess dough.
8. Brush the top with beaten egg to create the egg wash. Make a few small slits in the top to allow steam to escape.
9. Bake in the preheated oven for about 1 hour 30 minutes, or until the pastry is golden brown and the filling is cooked through.
10. If using aspic, dissolve gelatin in hot chicken stock according to package instructions and pour it into the steam vents as the pâté cools. This step is traditional but optional.
11. Allow the Pâté en Croûte to cool completely before chilling in the refrigerator. Slice and serve cold.

DIETARY MODIFICATIONS

Vegetarian: Substitute the meats with a combination of finely chopped mushrooms, lentils, and nuts for a rich, umami-packed filling. Replace chicken stock with vegetable stock for the aspic.

Vegan: Follow the vegetarian modifications and also substitute the pastry butter with a plant-based alternative. Use a flax or chia egg for binding the filling and omit the egg wash or use a non-dairy milk wash instead.

Gluten-Free: Use a gluten-free all-purpose flour blend instead of regular flour for the pastry and check that the brandy and other ingredients are gluten-free. Gluten-free gelatin or agar-agar can be used for the aspic.

INGREDIENT SPOTLIGHT: UNSALTED BUTTER

The spotlight ingredient for this recipe is the unsalted butter which plays a pivotal role in creating the rich, flaky pastry that characterizes a traditional Pâté en Croûte. Butter has been a staple in French cooking for centuries. Provided from churned cream, this dairy product not only delivers flavor but also contributes to the layers and pockets of air that puff during baking. Its use in pastries dates back to the Renaissance period, showcasing its enduring importance in creating the perfect crust.

CHEF'S TIPS

- Keep all pastry ingredients as cold as possible to ensure a flaky texture.
- Do not overwork the pastry dough, as this can result in a tough crust.
- Chill the filled pâté before baking to prevent the pastry from shrinking.
- Use a meat thermometer to check the internal temperature of the pâté, which should reach at least 160°F (71°C).
- Let the Pâté en Croûte set in the fridge overnight to fully develop the flavors and firm up for clean slicing.

POSSIBLE VARIATIONS OF THE RECIPE

- **Mixed Meat Pâté:** Incorporate veal or duck meat alongside the pork and chicken liver for a more complex flavor profile.
- **Festive Pâté:** Add pistachios and dried cranberries to the filling for a festive twist and a pop of color.
- **Spicy Pâté:** Introduce a blend of spices like espelette pepper or cayenne for added heat and a modern take on the classic recipe.

HEALTH NOTE & CALORIC INFORMATION

A traditional slice of Pâté en Croûte is quite rich in calories due to the buttery pastry and dense meat filling. A moderate slice would have approximately 600 to 800 calories, with significant amounts of protein and fat. Since this dish is intended to be savored in small portions as part of a larger spread or meal, enjoy it mindfully as part of a balanced diet.

LAVENDER HONEY CROISSANTS

The croissant is a staple of French cuisine, with its origins dating back to the 13th century. However, the use of lavender and honey in pastries introduces a Provençal twist to this classic pastry, making it a delightful blend of traditional French baking and the floral essence of the French countryside. Lavender is widely used in the Provence region for its fragrant and soothing qualities, pairing excellently with the natural sweetness of honey.

INGREDIENTS

- 1 cup warm whole milk (about 110°F)
- 1 tablespoon active dry yeast
- 3 tablespoons lavender honey
- 3 1/4 cups all-purpose flour, plus extra for dusting
- 1 tablespoon kosher salt
- 2 tablespoons dried culinary lavender
- 1 cup unsalted butter, chilled and cubed
- 1 large egg, for egg wash
- Coarse sugar for sprinkling (optional)

DIRECTIONS

1. Combine warm milk, yeast, and 1 tablespoon of lavender honey in a bowl. Allow it to stand for 5-10 minutes until yeast is active and foamy.
2. In a large mixing bowl, whisk together the flour and salt. Gradually add in the milk mixture and mix until a dough begins to form.
3. Transfer the dough to a floured surface and knead for 5 minutes until smooth. Cover with plastic wrap and let it rest for 30 minutes at room temperature.
4. While the dough is resting, prepare the butter. Place the butter between two sheets of parchment paper and pound it with a rolling pin into a 8x5 inch rectangle. Return to the refrigerator to keep chilled.
5. On a lightly floured surface, roll out the dough into a 16x10 inch rectangle. Place the chilled butter on half of the dough and fold the other half over the butter, sealing the edges.
6. Roll out the dough into a rectangle again, then fold it into thirds like a letter. Turn the dough 90 degrees and repeat the rolling and folding process twice more. If the dough becomes too soft or butter starts to ooze out, refrigerate it briefly.
7. Wrap the dough in plastic wrap and refrigerate for at least 1 hour or up to overnight.
8. Preheat the oven to 400°F (200°C). Line baking sheets with parchment paper.
9. Roll out the dough on a floured surface to a 1/4 inch thickness. Cut into triangles and sprinkle a little dried lavender on each.
10. Roll each triangle tightly from the base to the tip to form a croissant shape. Curve the ends to form a crescent.
11. Place the croissants on the prepared baking sheets. Mix the remaining 2 tablespoons of lavender honey with the egg to create an egg wash and brush this over the croissants. If desired, sprinkle with coarse sugar.
12. Bake for 15-20 minutes or until golden brown.

DIETARY MODIFICATIONS

Vegetarian: This recipe is already suitable for vegetarians.
Vegan: Replace whole milk with almond or soy milk, use a vegan butter substitute, and create a plant-based egg wash by combining almond milk with a tablespoon of maple syrup or agave nectar.
Lactose Intolerance: Substitute the whole milk with lactose-free milk and use lactose-free margarine instead of butter.

INGREDIENT SPOTLIGHT: LAVENDER HONEY

Lavender honey is the star ingredient here, hailing from the lavender fields of Provence, France. Lavender honey is harvested by bees that primarily gather nectar from lavender blossoms, which gives the honey a distinctive floral flavor and aroma. It's a natural sweetener that pairs well with various dishes and is perfect for baking due to its ability to withstand high temperatures without losing its flavor profile.

CHEF'S TIPS

- Keep all ingredients, especially butter and milk, chilled until use to maintain the flakiness of the dough.
- Work quickly when handling the dough to prevent the butter from melting, as this can affect layering.
- Ensure the yeast is fresh and active for the dough to rise appropriately; expired yeast can ruin the croissants.
- Be gentle when spreading the egg wash to avoid deflating the croissants.
- Allow croissants to cool on the baking sheet for a few minutes before transferring them to a wire rack to prevent them from becoming soggy.

POSSIBLE VARIATIONS OF THE RECIPE

- **Chocolate Lavender Croissants:** Add a small piece of dark chocolate to the center of each triangle before rolling.
- **Almond Lavender Croissants:** Sprinkle ground almonds along with dried lavender onto the dough before rolling and top with an almond glaze post-baking.
- **Savory Lavender Croissants:** Swap the honey for a lavender-infused olive oil and top with sea salt before baking for a savory version.

HEALTH NOTE & CALORIC INFORMATION

One lavender honey croissant typically contains:

- Calories: 280-350
- Fat: 16-22g
- Carbohydrates: 30-36g
- Protein: 5-7g
- Sugars: 5-9g
- Sodium: 290-360mg

This information may vary based on the size of the croissant and specific brands of ingredients used.

RATATOUILLE STUFFED PEPPERS

Ratatouille Stuffed Peppers is a delightful fusion that marries the classic French vegetable stew, Ratatouille, with a staple appetizer or side dish found in many world cuisines – the stuffed pepper. Ratatouille, hailing from Nice, has humble beginnings as a poor farmer's dish but has since risen to worldwide fame for its simplicity and robust flavors. This recipe takes the colorful medley of Mediterranean vegetables and nestles them into bell peppers, offering a beautiful presentation and a satisfying vegetarian meal.

INGREDIENTS

- 4 large bell peppers, assorted colors
- 2 small zucchinis, finely diced
- 1 small eggplant, finely diced
- 1 red onion, finely diced
- 2 cloves of garlic, minced
- 2 tomatoes, diced
- 1 yellow squash, finely diced
- 1 red bell pepper, finely diced (for the filling)
- 1/4 cup olive oil
- 2 tablespoons fresh basil, chopped
- 1 tablespoon fresh thyme, chopped
- 1 teaspoon sea salt
- 1/2 teaspoon black pepper
- 1/4 cup grated Parmesan cheese
- 1/4 cup breadcrumbs
- Fresh parsley for garnish

DIRECTIONS

1. Preheat your oven to 375°F (190°C).
2. Cut the tops off the 4 large bell peppers and remove the seeds and membranes. Set aside.
3. In a large skillet, heat the olive oil over medium heat. Add the diced red onion and garlic and sauté until translucent, about 3 minutes.
4. Add the zucchini, eggplant, yellow squash, and diced red bell pepper. Cook until the vegetables are tender but still have some bite, about 7-10 minutes.
5. Stir in the diced tomatoes, basil, and thyme. Season with salt and pepper. Cook for another 5 minutes, allowing the flavors to meld.
6. Mix in the breadcrumbs and half of the Parmesan cheese until well combined.
7. Fill each of the hollowed-out large bell peppers with the ratatouille filling. Place them upright in a baking dish.
8. Sprinkle the remaining Parmesan cheese over the tops of the stuffed peppers.
9. Bake in the preheated oven for approximately 25-30 minutes, until the peppers are tender and the tops are golden brown.
10. Garnish with fresh parsley before serving.

DIETARY MODIFICATIONS

Vegetarian: The recipe is already vegetarian-friendly.
Vegan: Replace the Parmesan cheese with nutritional yeast or a vegan cheese alternative, and use a vegan breadcrumb or simply omit it.
Gluten-Free: Use gluten-free breadcrumbs or substitute with ground almonds or gluten-free oats for the crunch.

INGREDIENT SPOTLIGHT: EGGPLANT

Eggplant is the spotlight ingredient. It's key to the distinctiveness of ratatouille, with its spongy texture that soaks up the delicious flavors of the herbs and olive oil. Known to have originated in India, eggplant spread to the Mediterranean and became synonymous with regional dishes like ratatouille. Its versatility in absorbing flavors makes it indispensable in this recipe.

CHEF'S TIPS

- Ensure that the eggplant and zucchini pieces are of a uniform size for even cooking.
- Salt the diced eggplant and let it sit for 10-15 minutes before cooking to draw out bitterness.
- Blanch the hollowed-out peppers in boiling water for 2-3 minutes for a softer texture upon baking.
- Customize the filling with additional herbs like rosemary or marjoram for an aromatic punch.
- Let the stuffed peppers sit for 5 minutes after baking for flavors to set.

POSSIBLE VARIATIONS OF THE RECIPE

- **Meat Lovers:** Add diced chorizo or pancetta to the sautéed vegetables for a smoky flavor.
- **Cheese Crust:** Mix grated Gruyère or mozzarella with the breadcrumbs for a cheesy, crispy topping.
- **Spicy Kick:** Incorporate chili flakes or diced chili peppers into the ratatouille for added heat.

HEALTH NOTE & CALORIC INFORMATION

A serving of Ratatouille Stuffed Peppers provides a good balance of vegetables, making it rich in dietary fiber, vitamins A and C, and potassium. The addition of Parmesan cheese offers protein and calcium, though it does increase the fat content. Each stuffed pepper is approximately 200-250 calories, with the variation depending on the size of the vegetables and the type of cheese used.

TRUFFLE MACARONI AND CHEESE

Macaroni and Cheese has its roots in the comfort cuisine of the American South but its origins are definitively European, first appearing in English cookbooks as far back as the 14th century. Our twist on this classic incorporates the luxury and depth of truffles—fungi highly prized since ancient times for their earthy and powerful aroma. The combination of creamy cheese sauce and the umami-rich truffle elevates a simple dish to a gourmet experience.

INGREDIENTS

- 1 pound elbow macaroni
- 3 tablespoons unsalted butter
- 3 tablespoons all-purpose flour
- 2 cups whole milk
- 1 cup heavy cream
- 1 tablespoon truffle oil
- 2 cups grated sharp cheddar cheese
- 1 cup grated Gruyere cheese
- 1/2 cup grated Parmesan cheese
- 1/2 teaspoon garlic powder
- 1/2 teaspoon onion powder
- 1/2 teaspoon mustard powder
- Salt and black pepper to taste
- 2 tablespoons chopped fresh truffles (optional)
- 1/2 cup panko breadcrumbs

DIRECTIONS

1. Preheat your oven to 350°F (175°C).
2. Cook the macaroni in a large pot of boiling salted water until just al dente, about 7 minutes. Drain well and set aside.
3. In the same pot, melt the butter over medium heat. Sprinkle in the flour and whisk constantly for about 1 minute to create a roux.
4. Slowly pour in the milk and heavy cream, whisking continuously to prevent lumps. Cook until the mixture thickens and coats the back of a spoon, about 5 minutes.
5. Lower the heat and stir in the truffle oil, cheddar cheese, Gruyere cheese, and Parmesan cheese until smooth. If using fresh truffles, reserve some for garnish and add the rest to the sauce now.
6. Season the sauce with garlic powder, onion powder, mustard powder, salt, and black pepper.
7. Add the cooked macaroni to the pot and stir until well coated with the cheese sauce.
8. Transfer the macaroni and cheese to a greased baking dish.
9. In a small bowl, toss the panko breadcrumbs with a bit of truffle oil and then sprinkle over the macaroni.
10. Bake for 25-30 minutes, until the top is golden brown and the sauce is bubbly.
11. Remove from the oven, let it cool slightly, and serve garnished with reserved chopped truffles if desired.

DIETARY MODIFICATIONS

Vegetarian: The recipe is already vegetarian. Simply ensure that the cheeses used are made without animal rennet.

Gluten-Free: Substitute the all-purpose flour with a gluten-free flour blend and use gluten-free macaroni. Ensure the panko breadcrumbs are also gluten-free.

Lactose-Intolerance: Replace the dairy components with lactose-free milk, lactose-free cream, and lactose-free cheeses if available. Be aware that this will alter the flavor slightly and might reduce the creaminess.

INGREDIENT SPOTLIGHT: TRUFFLE OIL

Truffle oil is the star of this dish. Derived from the highly coveted truffle fungi, truffle oil is usually olive oil or another carrier oil infused with truffles' unique flavor. Truffles have been a part of culinary traditions since ancient Greek and Roman times, symbolizing opulence and depth in food. Its strong flavor profiles are best used in moderation, but a small amount can transform a simple dish into a gourmet experience.

CHEF'S TIPS

- For the creamiest sauce, shred the cheese from a block rather than buying pre-shredded cheese, which can have additives that prevent clumping but also hinder melting.
- Incorporate the cheese into the sauce one handful at a time, allowing each addition to melt before adding more.
- Fresh truffles will give the dish an intense and authentic truffle flavor, but are a luxury. As an alternative, a high-quality truffle oil can also impart the signature earthy profile.
- Do not rinse the pasta after cooking as it helps the sauce cling to the macaroni.
- Allow the baked macaroni and cheese to rest for 5-10 minutes after removing it from the oven; this helps it set and prevents it from being runny.

POSSIBLE VARIATIONS OF THE RECIPE

- **Crabmeat Truffle Macaroni and Cheese:** For a seafood twist, fold in 8 ounces of lump crabmeat into the cheese sauce before adding the macaroni.
- **Bacon Truffle Macaroni and Cheese:** Enhance the savoriness by mixing in cooked, chopped bacon with the macaroni before baking.
- **Vegan Truffle Macaroni and Cheese:** Use a combination of cashew cream, nutritional yeast, and vegan cheeses to mimic the creamy sauce while incorporating truffle seasoning or oil for the signature flavor.

HEALTH NOTE & CALORIC INFORMATION

A single serving of Truffle Macaroni and Cheese is high in calories and fat due to the cheese, cream, and pasta. However, it's also very rich in calcium and can provide a good amount of protein. Estimated calories per serving (1/8th of the recipe): 560 kcal. This dish is best enjoyed as an occasional indulgence or in a smaller portion size as part of a balanced diet.

DECONSTRUCTED BEEF BOURGUIGNON

Traditional Beef Bourguignon, a French classic from the Burgundy region, typically involves simmering beef in red wine and beef stock, flavored with garlic, onions, and a bouquet garni, with pearl onions and mushrooms. It's a dish famously brought to the spotlight by Julia Child, conveying the essence of French country cooking. Our deconstructed version honors the original but presents it with a contemporary twist—each element is prepared separately and then artfully assembled, allowing for a fresh take on texture and presentation while maintaining the rich depth of flavor.

INGREDIENTS

- 800g beef chuck, cut into 2-inch cubes
- Sea salt and freshly ground black pepper, to taste
- 2 tbsp olive oil
- 1 bottle (750 ml) full-bodied red wine (preferably Burgundy)
- 2 cups beef stock
- 1 bouquet garni (thyme, bay leaf, and parsley tied together)
- 4 cloves garlic, minced
- 2 tbsp tomato paste
- 1 large onion, diced
- 2 carrots, cut into 1-inch pieces
- 150g pearl onions, peeled
- 250g button mushrooms, quartered
- 4 strips of bacon, cut into lardons
- 2 tbsp unsalted butter
- 1 tbsp all-purpose flour
- Fresh parsley, chopped (for garnish)

DIRECTIONS

1. Season the beef cubes with salt and pepper.
2. In a large pot, heat 1 tablespoon of olive oil over medium-high heat. Sear the beef cubes in batches until browned on all sides, then set aside.
3. Deglaze the pot with the red wine, scraping up the brown bits with a wooden spoon.
4. Add the seared beef back into the pot, along with the beef stock, bouquet garni, half of the minced garlic, tomato paste, diced onion, and carrots. Bring to a simmer.
5. Cover and gently simmer for 2-3 hours or until the beef is tender.
6. In the meantime, blanch the pearl onions in boiling water for 2 minutes, then shock in ice water. This will make them easier to peel.
7. Sauté the bacon lardons in a skillet until crisp. Transfer to a paper towel to drain.
8. In the same skillet, add 1 tablespoon of butter and the remaining minced garlic. Sauté the quartered mushrooms until browned. Remove and set aside.
9. Once the beef is tender, remove it from the pot and set aside. Strain the remaining liquid and reduce it by half to make a rich sauce.
10. In a separate skillet, melt the remaining 1 tablespoon of butter and whisk in the flour to make a roux. Cook for 2 minutes until golden brown.
11. Slowly whisk the reduced sauce into the roux to thicken it. Adjust seasoning as needed.
12. Assemble the dish by placing beef cubes on a plate, and artfully arrange the carrots, pearl onions, mushrooms, and bacon around the beef.
13. Drizzle the thickened sauce over the beef and garnish with freshly chopped parsley.

DIETARY MODIFICATIONS

Vegetarian: Substitute beef with portobello mushrooms, cut into thick slices, and use vegetable stock instead of beef stock. The deep flavors of portobello offer a meaty texture and umami-rich taste.

Vegan: Along with the vegetarian substitutions, use olive oil instead of butter, and skip the bacon. Crisp-fried shallots can make a great topping for added crunch and flavor.

Gluten-Free: Simply replace the all-purpose flour with cornstarch or your favorite gluten-free flour to make the roux for the sauce.

INGREDIENT SPOTLIGHT: RED WINE

Red Wine, more specifically Burgundy, is the spotlight ingredient in this dish. Originating from the Burgundy region in France, a good Burgundy is known for its deep flavor profile, which adds a complex richness to the stew. Wine has been used in cooking for centuries, both for its ability to tenderize meat and for the robust flavor it imparts. When cooked, the alcohol in wine evaporates, leaving behind a concentrated flavor that is key in creating the iconic taste of Beef Bourguignon.

CHEF'S TIPS

- Pat the beef dry before searing to ensure the perfect caramelization.
- Cook the beef in batches to avoid overcrowding and steaming instead of searing.
- Use a wine you enjoy drinking, as its flavor becomes more pronounced during cooking.
- Be careful not to overcook the mushrooms and pearl onions; they should retain some texture.
- Let the Beef Bourguignon rest for a few minutes after plating, then serve with crusty bread to soak up the delicious sauce.

POSSIBLE VARIATIONS OF THE RECIPE

- **Fall-Apart Tender:** Cook the beef sous-vide at 55°C for 24 hours before searing for unrivaled tenderness.
- **Spicy Twist:** Add a teaspoon of smoked paprika and a pinch of cayenne pepper to the sauce to introduce some smoky heat.
- **Creamy Sauce:** Introduce a touch of heavy cream to the reduced sauce for a more indulgent, velvety texture.

HEALTH NOTE & CALORIC INFORMATION

This deconstructed version retains the indulgent qualities of the original, with a balanced composition of protein, fats, and carbohydrates. A serving holds approximately 600–800 calories, with the richness of the dish coming from the beef and the butter used in preparation. It is high in protein, providing essential amino acids, and contains various vitamins and minerals from the vegetables. However, it is also high in saturated fats and should be enjoyed in moderation within a balanced diet.

CARAMELIZED ONION
AND GOAT CHEESE TARTLETS

Originating from the quaint bistros of France, tartlets have been a staple in the appetizer world, seducing palates with their delicate crusts and versatile fillings. This recipe for Caramelized Onion and Goat Cheese Tartlets combines the sweet, sumptuous flavor of slowly caramelized onions with the tangy kick of goat cheese—a symphony of taste nested in a flaky, buttery shell. The interplay of the sweetness from the onions and the sharpness of the cheese make this elegant appetizer a party pleaser that carries a touch of rustic charm and fine dining finesse.

INGREDIENTS

- 1 sheet of puff pastry, thawed
- 3 tablespoons unsalted butter
- 3 medium yellow onions, thinly sliced
- 1 teaspoon granulated sugar
- 1 tablespoon balsamic vinegar
- 4 ounces goat cheese, room temperature
- 1 teaspoon fresh thyme leaves
- 1 egg, beaten (for egg wash)
- Salt and freshly ground black pepper to taste

DIRECTIONS

1. Preheat your oven to 375°F (190°C).
2. Roll out the thawed puff pastry on a lightly floured surface. Cut into rounds using a cookie cutter or the rim of a glass that fits your tartlet pans.
3. Place the puff pastry rounds into the individual tartlet pans, gently pressing to fit. Trim any overhang. Prick the bottoms with a fork. Chill in the fridge for about 15 minutes.
4. Meanwhile, melt butter in a large skillet over medium heat. Add the sliced onions and a pinch of salt. Cook, stirring occasionally, until onions are soft and golden brown, about 20 minutes.
5. Sprinkle the sugar over the onions and cook for another 5-7 minutes, until they are caramelized. Stir in the balsamic vinegar, cook for another 2 minutes, then remove from heat. Allow to cool slightly.
6. Take the pastry shells out of the fridge. Divide the caramelized onions among the shells.
7. Crumble goat cheese over the onions and sprinkle with thyme leaves. Season with salt and pepper.
8. Brush the edges of the pastry with the beaten egg.
9. Bake in the preheated oven for 20-25 minutes, or until the pastry is golden and puffed.
10. Allow to cool for a few minutes before removing from the tartlet pans. Serve warm or at room temperature.

DIETARY MODIFICATIONS

Gluten-Free: To make this recipe gluten-free, use a gluten-free puff pastry available at health food stores. Ensure all other ingredients are certified gluten-free.

Vegan: For a vegan version, substitute the butter with a plant-based butter, use a dairy-free puff pastry, and replace the goat cheese with a vegan cheese alternative that crumbles well. Omit the egg wash or use a plant-based milk wash.

Lactose Intolerant: Those with lactose intolerance can simply use lactose-free butter and a lactose-free hard cheese that's been crumbled or grated, such as aged cheddar or Parmesan, in place of goat cheese.

INGREDIENT SPOTLIGHT: GOAT CHEESE

Goat cheese, also known as chèvre, is the star of this recipe. It is made from the milk of goats and is cherished for its distinct, tart flavor and creamy texture. With a history tracing back thousands of years, goat cheese was likely one of the earliest made dairy products. It's packed with essential nutrients like vitamin A, vitamin B, riboflavin, calcium, iron, phosphorus, magnesium, and potassium. The tangy kick of goat cheese contrasts the sweetness of the onions, bringing balance and depth to the tartlets.

CHEF'S TIPS

- Make sure your puff pastry is cold but pliable to prevent shrinkage during baking.
- Caramelize the onions slowly; rushing the process can result in burnt onions, which would impart a bitter taste.
- Use room temperature goat cheese for easier crumbling and better texture in the finished tartlet.
- An egg wash gives a beautiful shine to the puff pastry, but be careful not to let it pool in the bottom of the tartlet.
- Allow the caramelized onions to cool slightly before placing on the puff pastry to prevent sogginess.

POSSIBLE VARIATIONS OF THE RECIPE

- **Mediterranean Flair:** Add chopped olives, sun-dried tomatoes, and a sprinkle of za'atar to the caramelized onion mixture for a Mediterranean twist.
- **Breakfast Tartlets:** Introduce finely chopped, cooked bacon or breakfast sausage, and top each tartlet with a quail egg before baking for a brunch-appropriate version.
- **Dessert Option:** Swap out the savory for sweet by topping the puff pastry with a thin layer of almond cream, thinly sliced pears, a drizzle of honey, and a sprinkle of powdered sugar instead of the onions and cheese.

HEALTH NOTE & CALORIC INFORMATION

Each tartlet (assuming 12 servings per recipe) contains approximately:

- Calories: 180
- Fat: 12g
- Carbohydrates: 15g

- Calories: 180
- Fat: 12g
- Carbohydrates: 15g

Note that variations in size and the brands of ingredients used may affect the nutritional values.

RUSTIC ROSEMARY AND SEA SALT BAGUETTE

This baguette recipe is a homage to the art of traditional French baking, flavored with rosemary—a herb cherished in the Mediterranean for its pungent aroma and pine-like flavor. Rosemary has graced European kitchens since the times of the ancient Greeks and Romans. Our baguette takes a classic French bread, noted for its crispy crust and chewy interior, and infuses it with the earthy tones of rosemary, topped off with a sprinkle of coarse sea salt for an extra crunch.

INGREDIENTS

- 4 cups bread flour, plus extra for dusting
- 1 tablespoon fresh rosemary, finely chopped
- 2 teaspoons active dry yeast
- 2 teaspoons sugar
- 1 ½ teaspoons sea salt, plus extra for topping
- 1 ¼ cups warm water
- 1 tablespoon olive oil, for greasing and brushing
- Cornmeal, for dusting

DIRECTIONS

1. In a large mixing bowl, combine the yeast, sugar, and warm water. Let it stand for 5 to 10 minutes or until it becomes foamy, indicating that the yeast is active.
2. Add 1 teaspoon of the sea salt and the chopped rosemary to the yeast mixture.
3. Gradually mix in the bread flour until a sticky dough forms.
4. Turn the dough out onto a floured surface and knead for about 10 minutes, until smooth and elastic. Add more flour as necessary to prevent sticking.
5. Shape the dough into a ball and place it in a bowl greased with olive oil, turning the dough to coat it evenly. Cover with plastic wrap or a damp cloth and let it rise in a warm place until doubled in size, about 1–1.5 hours.
6. Gently punch down the dough and divide it into 2 equal pieces. Shape each piece into a long, thin loaf, about 12 inches in length.
7. Place the loaves on a baking sheet that's been sprinkled with cornmeal to prevent sticking. Let the loaves rise again, uncovered, for about 30 minutes, or until puffy.
8. Preheat the oven to 450 degrees F (230 degrees C) with a baking stone or upside-down baking tray inside to heat.
9. Right before baking, slash the tops of the loaves 3–4 times diagonally using a sharp knife or lame. Brush the loaves lightly with olive oil and sprinkle them with a pinch of coarse sea salt.
10. Transfer the loaves onto the preheated stone or tray and bake for 20–25 minutes, or until they are golden brown and sound hollow when tapped on the bottom.
11. Remove the baguettes from the oven and let them cool on a wire rack before slicing. Serve warm or at room temperature.

DIETARY MODIFICATIONS

Gluten-Free: Substitute bread flour for a gluten-free flour mix designed for bread baking. Add 1 teaspoon of xanthan gum to the mix if it's not included in the gluten-free flour blend. Gluten-free doughs tend to be more sticky, so wet your hands when kneading.

Low-Sodium: Reduce the amount of regular sea salt in the dough to ¾ teaspoon and omit the extra sea salt topping. The bread will have subtle flavors complemented by the rosemary without the added saltiness.

Vegan: This recipe is inherently vegan, provided that you ensure the sugar source is vegan as some sugar is processed with animal bone char. Simply choose a vegan-certified sugar brand to ensure compliance.

INGREDIENT SPOTLIGHT: ROSEMARY

Rosemary is our standout ingredient. This aromatic evergreen herb not only imparts its distinctive flavor and aroma to dishes but also carries a history steeped in mythology and medicine. It was worn by Greek scholars to improve memory and used throughout the Middle Ages to ward off evil spirits. In the kitchen, rosemary is used in a variety of culinary dishes, from meats to breads, and is essential in our baguette recipe for its ability to add a depth of flavor that complements the rustic nature of this bread. In this application, it's finely chopped to distribute its flavor evenly throughout the loaf.

CHEF'S TIPS

- For a crispier crust, place a shallow pan of water at the bottom of the oven during preheating, and bake your baguettes with this steam.
- To ensure your yeast is active, make sure the water is warm but not hot to the touch; too hot, and it will kill the yeast.
- Proper slashing of the dough right before baking is not just cosmetic; it helps the bread expand evenly while cooking.
- When kneading the dough, use the heel of your hand to push the dough away, folding it back on itself, to develop the gluten strands essential for chewy bread.
- Don't slice into the baguette immediately after baking. Allowing it to cool slightly will enable the crust to set and prevent the bread from turning gummy.

POSSIBLE VARIATIONS OF THE RECIPE

- **Multigrain Baguette:** Incorporate a blend of whole wheat flour, oats, and flax seeds with the bread flour for a nutty and textured twist. Adjust hydration as whole grains tend to absorb more water.
- **Sun-Dried Tomato and Olive Baguette:** Add chopped sun-dried tomatoes and Kalamata olives into the dough after the first rise for a Mediterranean flavor explosion.
- **Sweet Provence Baguette:** Swap out the rosemary for herbes de Provence and mix in some dried lavender for a sweet, aromatic version that pairs beautifully with soft cheeses.

HEALTH NOTE & CALORIC INFORMATION

A typical rosemary and sea salt baguette made with the above-listed ingredients yields about 12 servings. Each serving contains approximately:

- Calories: 180-220 kcal
- Protein: 5-7 g
- Carbohydrates: 35-40 g
- Dietary Fiber: 1-2 g
- Sugars: 1 g
- Fat: 1-2 g
- Sodium: 290-360 mg

ESPRESSO CRÈME BRÛLÉE

Crème Brûlée, the quintessential French dessert, is known for its rich custard base and contrasting layer of hard caramel on top. While it traditionally features a vanilla custard, this Espresso Crème Brûlée version offers a robust twist, infusing the creamy classic with the complex and bold flavors of espresso. This marriage of French culinary elegance and the aromatic world of coffee creates a sophisticated dessert that's perfect for concluding a fancy dinner or simply indulging in a luxurious treat.

INGREDIENTS

- 2 cups heavy cream
- 1/4 cup granulated sugar, plus more for caramelizing
- 1/4 cup espresso or strong coffee, freshly brewed
- 1 vanilla bean, split and scraped, or 1 teaspoon vanilla extract
- 6 large egg yolks
- A pinch of salt

DIRECTIONS

1. Preheat your oven to 325°F (163°C).
2. In a medium saucepan, combine the heavy cream, vanilla bean (pod and seeds), and espresso. Warm the mixture over medium heat until it's hot but not boiling, then remove from heat and let it infuse for 15 minutes.
3. In a separate bowl, whisk the egg yolks, sugar, and salt together until the mixture becomes slightly paler in color.
4. Gradually pour the hot cream mixture into the egg yolks, whisking constantly. Strain the mixture through a fine sieve into a large jug or bowl to remove the vanilla pod and any large pieces of coffee bean.
5. Pour the custard mixture into ramekins placed in a baking dish. Fill the baking dish with hot water until it comes halfway up the sides of the ramekins.
6. Carefully place the baking dish in the preheated oven and bake for 40 to 45 minutes. The crème brûlée should be set but still a little wobbly in the center.
7. Remove the ramekins from the water bath and let them cool to room temperature. Then refrigerate for at least 2 hours, or until ready to serve.
8. Before serving, sprinkle a thin layer of granulated sugar over each custard, then caramelize the sugar using a kitchen torch or your oven's broiler until it's golden brown and hard. Serve immediately after caramelizing.

DIETARY MODIFICATIONS

Keto-Friendly: Substitute granulated sugar with a keto-friendly sweetener such as erythritol or monk fruit sweetener. Keep in mind that some sugar alternatives may not caramelize as well as sugar, so you may need to broil the tops a bit longer.

Lactose-Intolerant: Use lactose-free heavy cream or full-fat coconut milk as a substitute for regular heavy cream. The coconut milk will add a slight coconut flavor to the dish.

Vegan: To make a vegan version, substitute the heavy cream with canned full-fat coconut milk and replace the egg yolks with a mixture of silken tofu and cornstarch to thicken. Use a vegan sugar for caramelizing.

INGREDIENT SPOTLIGHT: ESPRESSO

Espresso is the spotlight ingredient in this recipe. Espresso is a concentrated form of coffee brewed by forcing a small amount of nearly boiling water under pressure through finely-ground coffee beans. Originating in Italy in the early 20th century, espresso is not only famed for its intense flavor and creamy consistency but also as the foundation of many types of coffee drinks. Espresso adds a deep, rich coffee flavor to the crème brûlée that complements the creamy custard.

CHEF'S TIPS

- For an even finer custard, leave your eggs out to come to room temperature before whisking with the sugar.
- When heating your cream, do not allow it to boil, as this can affect the smoothness of your custard.
- Baking the crème brûlée in a water bath ensures even, gentle cooking. Make sure the water comes up halfway up the ramekins for optimal heat distribution.
- Cooling the custards in the refrigerator for several hours or overnight will result in a firmer set, which contrasts beautifully with the brittle caramelized top.
- A kitchen torch is your best bet for achieving the perfect caramelized sugar topping. If using a broiler, watch closely to avoid burning the sugar.

POSSIBLE VARIATIONS OF THE RECIPE

- **Mocha Crème Brûlée:** Add 1 tablespoon of unsweetened cocoa powder to the cream mixture to introduce a chocolatey dimension to the espresso flavor.
- **Spiced Espresso Crème Brûlée:** Infuse the cream with not only espresso but also a cinnamon stick and a star anise for a warming, spiced version.
- **Irish Crème Brûlée:** Replace 1/4 cup of the heavy cream with Irish cream liqueur for a boozier and even more decadent dessert.

HEALTH NOTE & CALORIC INFORMATION

A typical serving size of Espresso Crème Brûlée contains approximately 300-400 calories, with the majority coming from fats in the heavy cream and the sugars used for both the custard and the caramelized topping. Given the richness of this dessert, it is best enjoyed in moderation, especially for those tracking their caloric intake.

ESCARGOT PUFFS WITH GARLIC BUTTER

Escargot, the French term for edible snails, is a delicacy dating back to ancient times, cherished by Roman emperors and French royalty alike. Often served as an appetizer in France, escargot is commonly prepared with garlic, butter, and parsley. Our recipe transforms this traditional dish into a chic pastry delight — Escargot Puffs with Garlic Butter. This fusion of classic French flavors enclosed within flaky puff pastry makes an elegant hors d'oeuvre, perfect for impressing guests at any soiree.

INGREDIENTS

- 24 canned snails (escargot), drained
- 1 sheet of frozen puff pastry, thawed
- 4 tablespoons unsalted butter, softened
- 2 garlic cloves, minced
- 2 tablespoons fresh parsley, finely chopped
- 1 small shallot, minced
- 1 teaspoon fresh lemon juice
- 1/4 teaspoon salt
- 1/4 teaspoon black pepper
- 1/4 teaspoon ground nutmeg
- 1 egg, beaten (for egg wash)
- Flour (for dusting)

DIRECTIONS

1. Preheat your oven to 375°F (190°C) and line a baking sheet with parchment paper.
2. In a mixing bowl, combine softened butter, minced garlic, chopped parsley, minced shallot, lemon juice, salt, pepper, and nutmeg. Mix until it forms a homogeneous garlic herb butter.
3. Lightly flour your working surface, and gently unfold the puff pastry sheet.
4. Using a rolling pin, lightly roll out the pastry to even out any creases and to slightly increase its surface area.
5. Cut the puff pastry into 24 equally-sized squares.
6. Place a small amount of garlic herb butter in the center of each puff pastry square.
7. Top the butter with one escargot and fold the pastry over it, pinching the edges to seal the puff. You should aim for a small pouch or a half-moon shape.
8. Move each puff to the prepared baking sheet, ensuring they are not touching each other.
9. Brush each puff lightly with beaten egg to give it a golden color upon baking.
10. Bake for 12-15 minutes, or until puffs are golden brown and have puffed up.
11. Remove from the oven and let cool for a few minutes before serving warm.

DIETARY MODIFICATIONS

Vegetarian: Swap the escargot for sautéed mushrooms finely chopped with a hint of soy sauce to mimic the umami flavor of snails. Keep the rest of the recipe the same.

Vegan: Along with the vegetarian modification, use vegan puff pastry and a blend of olive oil, nutritional yeast, and a pinch of turmeric instead of butter and egg wash to maintain color and richness.

Lactose Intolerance: Use lactose-free margarine or a plant-based butter substitute in place of regular butter. Ensure the puff pastry is lactose-free as well, as some brands use butter.

INGREDIENT SPOTLIGHT: SNAILS

The spotlight falls on the snail itself in this dish. Escargot is harvested primarily from land snail species like Helix pomatia and Helix aspersa. Considered a delicacy, escargot has been a part of gourmet European dining for centuries. Beyond its unique, subtly earthy flavor profile, snails are also known for their health benefits, being rich in protein and low in fat. Escargot is key to this recipe because it provides an irreplaceable depth of flavor that is central to the dish's identity.

CHEF'S TIPS

- Make sure to drain the canned escargot well to prevent the puff pastry from becoming soggy.
- Avoid overworking the puff pastry to ensure it remains light and flaky. Keep it cold and work quickly.
- Be sparse with the filling to prevent burst seams during baking.
- Ensure each puff is sealed tightly to keep the tasty filling inside and create a good puff.
- Serve immediately after baking for the best texture and flavor experience.

POSSIBLE VARIATIONS OF THE RECIPE

- **Herb Infusion:** Experiment with different herbs such as thyme, rosemary, or tarragon to infuse the butter with various flavors.
- **Cheese Invasion:** Add a small cube of gruyere or brie inside each puff with the snail for a gooey, cheesy experience.
- **Spicy Adventure:** Introduce a bit of heat with a sprinkle of finely chopped chili or a dash of cayenne pepper mixed into the garlic butter.

HEALTH NOTE & CALORIC INFORMATION

This appetizer offers a good balance of protein and carbs, with moderate fat due to the butter. By using unsalted butter and controlling the salt content, sodium levels can be managed. A serving size of two puffs provides approximately:

- Calories: 150-170
- Protein: 4-6 g
- Carbohydrates: 10-12 g
- Fat: 10-12 g
- Sodium: 150-200 mg
- Cholesterol: 25-35 mg

The exact nutritional values can vary based on the size of the pastries and the amount of filling used.

MINI CHOCOLATE SOUFFLÉS

The soufflé, with its delicate rise and rich flavor, is a pinnacle of French culinary prowess. Originating in the early 18th century, it has been a symbol of elegance in dining. Chocolate, once a luxurious item, became widespread in France in the 1600s. When it met the soufflé technique, the Mini Chocolate Soufflé was born—a divine marriage of technique and indulgence, perfect for impressing dinner guests or treating oneself to a bite of decadent history.

INGREDIENTS

- 6 ounces high-quality dark chocolate (at least 70% cacao)
- 3 large eggs, room temperature, separated
- 1/3 cup granulated sugar
- 2 tablespoons unsalted butter, plus extra for greasing the ramekins
- 1 teaspoon pure vanilla extract
- 1/4 teaspoon cream of tartar
- Powdered sugar for dusting (optional)
- Fresh berries for garnish (optional)

DIRECTIONS

1. Preheat your oven to 375°F (190°C), and position an oven rack in the lower third portion of the oven.
2. Grease four 8-ounce ramekins with butter, and coat the inside with a sprinkle of granulated sugar, tapping out the excess.
3. Melt the chocolate and butter together in a heatproof bowl set over a pot of simmering water (double boiler method), stirring until smooth. Remove from heat.
4. Stir in the vanilla extract and let the chocolate mixture cool slightly.
5. With an electric mixer, beat the egg whites on medium speed until frothy. Add the cream of tartar, then gradually add granulated sugar and increase the speed, continuing to beat until stiff peaks form.
6. Gently fold one-third of the beaten egg whites into the chocolate mixture to lighten it. Carefully fold in the remaining egg whites until no white streaks remain.
7. Spoon the mixture into the prepared ramekins, filling almost to the top. Level the tops with a knife or spatula.
8. Bake for 12-15 minutes, until the soufflés have risen with a slight jiggle in the center. Serve immediately, garnished with powdered sugar and fresh berries if desired.

DIETARY MODIFICATIONS

Gluten-Free: This recipe is naturally gluten-free, however, always double-check your chocolate and vanilla extract for any hidden gluten-containing additives.

Vegan: Replace the eggs with aquafaba (the liquid from a can of chickpeas). Use 6 tablespoons aquafaba and 1/4 teaspoon cream of tartar to make vegan meringue. Opt for vegan chocolate and substitute butter with a dairy-free alternative.

Lactose Intolerance: Select a dairy-free chocolate and use a lactose-free butter or margarine instead of regular butter. The other ingredients in the recipe are naturally lactose-free.

INGREDIENT SPOTLIGHT: DARK CHOCOLATE

Dark chocolate is not just a component of this recipe—it's the star. With its origins in Mesoamerican cultures, chocolate was a beverage exclusively for the elite. After reaching Europe, it evolved into the solid form we're familiar with today. In this recipe, at least 70% cacao chocolate not only provides a robust depth of flavor but also antioxidants. It's the magic element that, when melted, gives the soufflés their rich, indulgent taste, and it works beautifully to both flavor and solidify the soufflés.

CHEF'S TIPS

- Ensure your eggs are at room temperature to achieve maximum volume when whipped.
- Do not open the oven door while the soufflés are baking to prevent them from falling.
- When folding the egg whites into the chocolate mixture, use a gentle hand to keep the air in the meringue intact.
- Fill the ramekins to the right level to allow for a perfect rise—too little and they won't puff up, too much and they can overflow.
- Serve soufflés promptly after baking for the best texture and presentation.

POSSIBLE VARIATIONS OF THE RECIPE

- **Mocha Soufflés:** Add a teaspoon of instant espresso powder to the melted chocolate mixture for a subtle coffee flavor that complements the chocolate.
- **Spiced Chocolate Soufflés:** Stir 1/4 teaspoon of cinnamon and a pinch of cayenne pepper into the chocolate mixture before incorporating the egg whites for a warm, spicy twist.
- **Orange Chocolate Soufflés:** Infuse the melted butter with the zest of one orange for a citrus note, and replace vanilla extract with orange liqueur.

HEALTH NOTE & CALORIC INFORMATION

A typical Mini Chocolate Soufflé made with 70% cacao chocolate contains approximately 290 calories, with 18g of fat, 25g of carbohydrates, and 6g of protein. This treat is also a source of iron and fiber. However, calorie content can vary based on specific ingredient choices and serving sizes.

NIÇOISE SALAD ROLLS WITH AHI TUNA

Evoking the flavors of France's Côte d'Azur, this recipe intertwines the classic Niçoise salad with the elegance of sushi-inspired presentation. The Niçoise salad, originating from Nice, is known for its vibrant colors and fresh taste, typically featuring tomatoes, hard-boiled eggs, Niçoise olives, and anchovies or tuna. By introducing the concept of a roll, we pay homage to this traditional dish while adding an innovative, hands-on dining experience.

INGREDIENTS

- 8 rice paper wrappers
- 8 oz Ahi tuna, sushi-grade
- 4 cups mixed salad greens (such as baby spinach, arugula, and radicchio)
- 2 ripe tomatoes, sliced into half-moons
- 1 small red onion, thinly sliced
- 1/2 cup Niçoise olives, pitted and halved
- 4 hard-boiled eggs, sliced
- 8 small red potatoes, boiled and sliced
- 2 tbsp capers
- Fresh basil leaves
- Olive oil (for drizzle)
- Salt and pepper to taste
- Balsamic glaze (optional, for garnish)

DIRECTIONS

1. **Prep Vegetables & Tuna:** Start by preparing all the vegetables and the hard-boiled eggs as described in the ingredients list. For the Ahi tuna, cut it into long, thin strips around 1/2-inch thick.
2. **Blanch Potatoes:** Boil the small red potatoes until fork-tender, then slice them.
3. **Soften Rice Paper:** Fill a large plate or pie dish with warm water. Submerge a rice paper wrapper for about 20-30 seconds or until it is just soft and pliable.
4. **Assemble Rolls:** Lay the softened rice paper flat on a clean surface. In the center, place a small handful of mixed greens, a couple of slices of tomatoes, onions, and a few olive halves. Add a slice of hard-boiled egg, 1-2 slices of boiled potatoes, and sprinkle with some capers and a few leaves of fresh basil.
5. **Add Ahi Tuna:** Place a strip of Ahi tuna on top of the vegetables.
6. **Roll it Up:** Fold the bottom half of the rice paper wrapper over the filling. Then fold in the sides and continue to roll tightly. The wrapper will stick to itself and seal the roll. (*Repeat this process with the remaining wraps.)
7. **Serve:** Drizzle olive oil over the rolls, season with salt and pepper, and if desired, garnish with a balsamic glaze.
8. **Enjoy:** Serve immediately as a fresh, innovative take on the classic Niçoise salad.

DIETARY MODIFICATIONS

Vegetarian: Skip the Ahi tuna and substitute with grilled halloumi cheese or extra firm tofu. Ensure the tofu is well-pressed and perhaps marinated in a mixture akin to what you'd use for traditional tuna to retain the depth of flavor.

Vegan: Omit both Ahi tuna and eggs. Introduce chickpeas or marinated tempeh as protein sources, and consider adding avocado slices for creaminess and richness.

Gluten-Free: This recipe is inherently gluten-free, but be mindful of cross-contamination if gluten is a severe concern, and check that your balsamic glaze (if using) is certified gluten-free.

INGREDIENT SPOTLIGHT: AHI TUNA

Ahi Tuna: Ahi, also known as yellowfin tuna, is most familiar to the culinary world in its raw form, particularly in sashimi and poke bowls. It's cherished for its mildly sweet flavor and its firm texture. When purchasing Ahi, it's crucial to look for sushi-grade to ensure it's safe to consume raw. Ahi Tuna became an important ingredient in Western gastronomy thanks to its rich flavor and prestigious status. It's a rich source of protein and Omega-3 fatty acids.

CHEF'S TIPS

- When softening rice paper wrappers, it is best not to oversoak them as they can become tearable and challenging to handle.
- Use a sharp knife when slicing the Ahi tuna to ensure clean cuts without tearing the flesh.
- Rolling the salad rolls can be tricky at first — don't overfill, and maintain a firm but gentle pressure to ensure the roll stays together without squeezing out the fillings.
- To keep the rice paper wraps from sticking to each other or the surface, consider working on a damp kitchen towel and having another one handy to cover the finished rolls.
- Preparing the ingredients in an assembly line fashion can be an efficient way to make multiple rolls in a shorter timeframe.

POSSIBLE VARIATIONS OF THE RECIPE

- **Mediterranean Flair:** Introduce feta cheese, cucumber, and a hint of oregano to the rolls, creating a Greek salad-inspired version.
- **Spicy Asian Twist:** Add a spicy element with wasabi or sriracha mayo drizzled inside the rolls and substitute the olives for pickled ginger for an Asian fusion experience.
- **Meaty Makeover:** For a more substantial roll, add thinly sliced smoked duck breast or prosciutto in place of Ahi tuna.

HEALTH NOTE & CALORIC INFORMATION

Niçoise Salad Rolls with Ahi Tuna are a well-balanced dish high in protein, vitamins, and healthy fats. A typical roll (1/8 of the recipe) is around 200-250 calories, with the Ahi tuna contributing a good portion of the calories coming from protein. The olives and olive oil provide healthy monounsaturated fats. This meal is rich in dietary fiber and is a good source of Vitamin A (from the greens) and Vitamin C (from the tomatoes). If you have a balsamic glaze, be mindful of added sugars which can increase the calorie content slightly.